THE ROAD TO ROME

THE ROAD TO ROME

BY

ROBERT EMMET SHERWOOD

"All the roads of our neighbourhood were cheerful
and friendly having each of them pleasant qualities
of their own; but this one seemed different from the
others in its masterful suggestion of a serious purpose, speeding you along with a strange uplifting
of the heart."
—From "The Roman Road" in Kenneth
Grahame's "The Golden Age."

CHARLES SCRIBNER'S SONS

NEW YORK · LONDON

1927

TO
MY WIFE

PREFACE

(WITH FAIRLY COPIOUS REMARKS ON THE HIS-
TORICAL BACKGROUND OF THE PLAY)

In the year 323 B. C., Alexander the Great
died on a soft bed in Babylon, and the sun of empire, following its appointed course, moved west-
ward.

Babylon and Nineveh, Persepolis and Thebes,
Athens and Sparta, had risen and fallen—and as
the sun advanced their glory was dimmed in the
lengthening shadows.

Two new cities, colonies from the older states
to the eastward, had appeared in the center of the
Mediterranean world, had prospered and were
powerful. One was Carthage; the other was
Rome. It was a foregone conclusion that these
two states, rivals in commerce and in the avid
desire for expansion, would arrive ultimately at
each other's throats.

Carthage, situated on the north coast of Africa
directly across from Sicily, had been founded
originally by the active Phœnicians—the Canaan-
ites of the Bible—whose talents for trading impelled them to seek new sources of revenue, new
ports of call, in distant places. They developed,

in Carthage, an enormous base for expeditions to
Sicily, Sardinia, Spain, the Baleares and Malta,
and even into the rich and unknown interior of
Africa.

Eventually, Carthage outgrew its mother city,
Tyre, and became an independent state. Great
numbers of Greeks, Egyptians, and Lybians were
gathered into its huge population; but the blood
of its governing class, and the general character
of its civilization, remained essentially Phœnician.

Originally a monarchy, Carthage developed
into an oligarchic democracy, organized on lines
similar to the Spartan system; but where prestige
in Sparta depended on physical prowess and pro-
ficiency in the arts of war, in Carthage it depended almost entirely upon wealth. Money, indeed, was the supreme power in this last outpost
of Semitic civilization; there was always plenty
of it on hand, and a great deal more being brought
in constantly by caravans and fleets.

Carthage became rich and flabby. Its citizens,
like all rich men, took a mild interest in the arts,
but never managed to create anything of endur-
ing importance; Carthaginian art, like the later
Roman art, was borrowed from Greece, from
Egypt, and from the Orient.

The Carthaginians displayed a Babylonian
taste for luxury and magnificence and, in the
worship of their gods, for orgiastic decadence.

In "Salambo," Flaubert describes the wild, un-
bridled revelries in Carthage with the same affec-
tion for minute detail that he displays in his dis-
sections of the home life of Emma Bovary.

There must have been a few men of Spartan
mould in Carthage—the records of Hamilcar's
and Hannibal's armies provide sufficient evidence
of that; but their countrymen, in general, were
undoubtedly a feeble, degenerate lot. The Romans, on the other hand, were an energetic, seri-
ous-minded, frugal people, with an absurdly
exaggerated sense of duty. They had no time for
philosophy and art, and they entertained a supreme contempt for the Athenian Greeks who had
frittered away their lives in the pursuit of such
frivolous pastimes.

Carthage, then, was on the decline; Rome was
on the make.

Sicily became the first bone of contention for
Romans and Carthaginians to pick at. Carthage
controlled Sicily and Rome wanted it, and the two
states decided to argue the matter out in battle.
(The Roman excuse was that Sicily should be delivered from the Carthaginian yoke, but that was
an old one, even then).

The First Punic War started in 264 B. C., and
lasted for twenty-three years. It was a long,
bitter, bloody and generally inconclusive struggle, in which Rome appeared, for the first time,

as a naval power.   Although the victories and the
losses were about evenly divided, Carthage's
previously undisputed supremacy on the sea was
destroyed.

Peace treaties were signed in 240, giving Rome
an entirely unearned control over Sicily.   Subsequently, Rome sent its quinqueremes and triremes
to seize Corsica and Sardinia, but the indolent
politicians in Carthage made no official attempt
to show that they resented this unwarranted act.

There was one Carthaginian, however, who
emerged from the First Punic War with a con-
suming hatred of his Roman enemies and an un-
quenchable desire for revenge.   This was Hamilcar, surnamed Barca (the lightning), who had
won a brilliant series of victories on land in the
last years of the war.

Hamilcar took it upon himself to punish Rome,
and to wipe out the stain on Carthaginian honor
that had been imposed by the disgraceful treaties.   Sicily, Sardinia, and Corsica became his Al-
sace-Lorraine.   He gained control of the war
party in Carthage, a party which had the active
support, strangely enough, of the proletariat.
His opponents, the members of the peace party,
were the elders of the state, led by Hanno, who
realized that war with Rome was expensive,
strenuous and calculated to interfere with their
elaborate pleasures.

Hanno and the others were not strong enough
to subdue the vigorous Hamilcar, and in 236 he
raised an enormous army and navy and sailed for
Spain, to establish a new Phœnician empire on
the western edge of the Mediterranean world. In
a series of brilliant campaigns, he managed to
subdue the refractory Iberian tribes south of the
river Ebro and to establish Carthage as the
supreme power in that region.

Hamilcar saw, in Spain, the basis for larger
and far more ambitious operations; his thoughts
and his hopes travelled continually beyond the
Pyrenees, beyond the Alps, to the gates of Rome,
where his overwhelming hatred might find final
satisfaction. But it was not for Hamilcar to
realize his expansive ambitions; in 228 he was
killed in battle, and the command passed to his
son-in-law, Hasdrubal, who was of a more concil-
iatory disposition. Hasdrubal effected treaties
with the Romans, by which Spain was divided into
two "spheres of influence" (to employ the elegant
phrase of modern diplomacy); Carthage was to
remain in the south and Rome in the north, with
the Ebro as a boundary.

In 220, Hasdrubal was assassinated (it is possible that Hanno's peace party in Carthage had
a hand in this murder; Hanno always envied the
popularity of the Barca family). The command
of the armies then passed to Hamilcar's eldest

son, Hannibal, and to him was entrusted the fulfillment of his father's hopes.

Hannibal is a unique figure in history—a sad, lonely and utterly baffling character. He was a brilliant soldier; his actual accomplishments prove that beyond all question. But of his qualities as a man, his habits, his beliefs, his philosophy, nothing definitely is known, nor ever will be known. With the exception of Archimedes, who was killed by the Romans in the siege of Syracuse, there was not one great mind in the world in Hannibal's time—no one who was qualified to appraise the true character of the conquering Carthaginian and to place it on file in the records of humanity. The student, however, is always at liberty to guess about Hannibal— and the play that is published herewith is the dramatization of a guess.

In his book on Hannibal, William O'Connor Morris has this to say: "We do not possess a letter or a dispatch of this extraordinary man; we have no Carthaginian records to tell us what he was; we know of him only from the reports of his enemies, who, while they could not deny his powers, feared and hated him through a succession of centuries. Yet enough remains to enable history to assert that he was a mighty genius in his camp, and in council; that . . . he has certainly not been surpassed as a warrior; that he was gifted with marvellous diplomatic skill, and with rare political insight; above all, that he was a single-minded patriot, apparently without one selfish thought, and devoted, throughout an heroic life, to the cause of his country, spite of base ingratitude, and half-hearted cowardice at home. Hannibal, too, was one of the greatest leaders of men who have ever been seen on the stage of events; he ruled an army of many races and tongues, whether in victory or defeat, with absolute sway; he maintained a protracted and ultimately hopeless contest for years, by the sheer force of his genius."

Hannibal's achievements in battle speak for themselves; his masterpieces of strategy at Lake Trasimenus and at Cannæ are still studied by budding officers at Sandhurst and West Point. Napoleon, who admired him intensely and attempted to emulate him in many ways, described Hannibal as "the most audacious of all, the most amazing, perhaps—so sturdy, so sure, so great in everything—who, at the age of twenty-six, conceived that which is hardly conceivable, accomplished that which can be considered impossible."

Behind his victories in the field, however, is the character of Hannibal himself. The Romans represented him as cruel, perfidious, treacherous. Livy, as a patriotic Roman historian, did his

best to emphasize Hannibal's brutality and to de-
precate his powers as a soldier. But even through
Livy's attempts at belittlement there glows the
light of genuine greatness. Those who study
Hannibal's career most closely can't fail to believe that he was a gentleman in an age when
gentlemen were rare and, in the main, unpopular.
As Mommsen says, "Though anger and envy and
meanness have written his history, they have not
been able to smear the spotless and noble image
it presents."

Hannibal was born in 247, during the dark
days of the First Punic War, arriving on earth
at a time when "the evil side of life was upper-
most," when "the red eyes of the ancestral ape
had come back into the world. It was a time
when reasonable men were howled down or mur-
dered," when "the western world was indeed black
with homicidal mania." *

His childhood was filled with the talk of battles
in which his father had butchered thousands of
Romans; the forces of death and destruction con-
stituted his heritage. Before Hamilcar sailed for
Spain, he laid his young son on the altar of Ba-al
and swore him to an oath of undying hatred of
Rome. That oath became Hannibal's life; he
could never forget it, never relax his incredible
efforts to carry it through. For fifty years he

* H. G. Wells, "The Outline of History," Book V, § 5.

struggled, valiantly and hopelessly, to stamp out the spreading fires of Roman supremacy.

He never accomplished his purpose; he saw the gates of Rome, but he did not shatter them. In the hour of his greatest victory, he turned from the goal toward which his father had pointed him, and marched away—to occupy a strange place in history as the triumphant leader of a lost cause.

Hamilcar took Hannibal to Spain and brought him up in the camps—training him, disciplining him, accustoming him to the heroism and the knavery, the glory and the ugliness, of war; with the result that, when Hannibal succeeded to the command, he was already an old, old soldier.

The peace party was still active in Carthage, under the leadership of Hanno, who made a determined effort to prevent Hannibal's succession. Hanno believed that Carthage had had enough of the embattled Barcides, and he urged his case earnestly before the Senate—giving voice to these prophetic words: "I am of the opinion that this youth should be kept at home . . . lest at some time or other this small fire should kindle a vast conflagration." Later, when Hannibal was about to follow the line of his father's vision across the Pyrenees, Hanno again addressed the Senate: "You, supplying as it were fuel to the flames, have sent to your armies a youth burning with the desire of sovereign power, and seeing *but one road to his object.*"

Hanno's protests were of no avail, and Hannibal was encouraged by his countrymen to go on with the costly but potentially profitable work of eliminating Rome as a competitive power. In this, it can hardly be said that the Carthaginians were actuated by any motives of altruistic patriotism (if, indeed, there is such a thing); they wanted to make the world safe for oligarchy. Furthermore, Hamilcar and Hasdrubal had sent enormous quantities of booty to Carthage as a result of their conquests in Spain, and there was every reason to believe that Hannibal could be trusted to continue the supply. The members of the Barca family were regarded, by their countrymen, as brilliant travelling salesmen, whose expense accounts were staggering but who managed to keep the home office well supplied with tremendous orders.

Hasdrubal—more of a statesman than a soldier—had pacified and co-ordinated the Iberian tribes and consolidated Carthage's power in Spain. Moreover, he had bequeathed to Hannibal a large, well-organized and well-equipped army. There remained no tasks in Southern Spain for Hannibal to complete.

Beyond the Ebro, however, lay Rome—and when raiding parties from Saguntum crossed the

river and attempted to plunder the Carthaginian
territory, Hannibal was given the opportunity to
strike back. The treaties had become scraps of
paper, and Hannibal was only too glad to recognize them as such.

He advanced northward, across the Ebro, and
laid siege to Saguntum, a large and prosperous
city, which was, nominally, under the protection
of Rome. The siege lasted for eight gory
months, during which time Rome offered no assistance whatever to the beleaguered Saguntines;
at last, the Carthaginians broke through the walls
and, after several days of violent fighting in the
streets, demolished the city.

When news of this disaster reached Rome, its
citizens were inflamed with righteous indignation
and, it must be admitted, with a certain uncom-
fortable sense of apprehension. A delegation,
headed by Quintus Fabius Maximus, an elderly
and dignified statesman, was despatched to
Carthage to demand the surrender of Hannibal,
dead or alive, that he might be punished for his
flagrant violation of Saguntine "neutrality."

Hanno was perfectly willing to agree to Fabius's demands, but other leaders in Carthage
were less docile. Fabius then delivered one of the
many dramatic gestures that have enlivened Roman history; gathering up his robe, he announced
that he held in it peace and war, and that Car-

thage might choose between them. The Carthaginians refused to accept the responsibility of such a choice, and Fabius, interpreting this as an affront, declared war.

So, in 218, the Second Punic War started— "the most memorable of all wars that were ever waged." *

Hannibal was ready for his supreme effort; on hearing of the decision that had emerged from the toga of Fabius Maximus, he started forward along the "one road to his object." His men, well trained and experienced in the Spanish campaigns, had been given long leaves of absence during the preceding winter, and were prepared for the ordeal. "Even the common soldier whose military instincts lengthened war had developed, felt the clear perception and the steady hand of his leader, and followed him with steadfast confidence to the unknown and distant land." †

Hannibal left his younger brother, Hasdrubal,‡ in command of the Carthaginian forces in Spain. The youngest of Hamilcar's sons, Mago, accom-

* Livy, Book XXI.

† Mommsen, Book III, Chap. 4.

‡ Note.—The apparent sparsity of given names in Carthage provokes some confusion as to the identities of various characters of this period. For example, there were at least eight men of prominence who bore the name "Hasdrubal." The first was Hamilcar's son-in-law, who succeeded Hamilcar and preceded Hannibal as commander-in-chief. The second (referred to above) was the second son of Hamilcar. A third Hasdrubal, who appears

panied Hannibal on his march, the other princi-
pal officers of the expeditionary force being Hasdrubal, Maharbal, Carthalo, Monomachus, and
Hanno (who is not to be confused with the leader
of the peace party).

In the Pyrenees, many of Hannibal's Spanish
troops became terrified at the prospect of more
and higher mountains, and deserted. Unable to
prevent this, Hannibal immediately sent back
some 10,000 men to the Carthaginian base in
Spain, as a means of convincing his army that
victory was easily obtainable.

With approximately eighty thousand infantry,
twelve thousand cavalry and forty elephants he
proceeded on into Gaul, conciliated the local
chieftains and marched with no great delays to
Avignon, on the Rhone. There he encountered
formidable difficulties: the Gauls, who were formed
in great numbers on the opposite bank, were
openly hostile; from the south came word that
Publius Cornelius Scipio, the Roman consul, had
landed at Massilia (Marseilles) with a large army
and was preparing to meet the Carthaginians at
the earliest possible moment.

Hannibal constructed boats and rafts with the

as a character in "The Road to Rome," was the leader of the
Numidian cavalry in Hannibal's army and probably the finest of
his officers. He, apparently, was no relation to the Barca family.
Still another, Hasdrubal Hædus, belonged to Hanno's peace party;
his name, translated literally, means "Hasdrubal the Kid."

scanty materials at hand, and used these to ferry
his animals and his equipment across the river.
Most of the soldiers, piling their arms and armor
on the rafts, swam across the swift-moving
stream.

No one knows just how the passage of the poor,
fat, bewildered elephants was managed. Livy
cites a story to the effect that the head keeper of
the elephants managed to tease the most ferocious
of them into a state of furious rage; the keeper
then plunged into the stream and swam hastily
across, with all the elephants puffing and snorting
after him. This, if true, must be listed among the
great comic moments of history.

It is more probable, says Livy reluctantly, that
the elephants were transported on rafts. The
Roman army, arriving on the scene later, discovered several huge rafts, one of which was two
hundred and fifty feet long by fifty wide.

The angry Gauls were disposed of by means of
a typical strategic trick (the Romans complained
much of Hannibal's "Punic perfidy"). Before
starting to ford the river, Hannibal sent Hanno
with a cavalry detachment a few miles upstream,
with orders to cross the river as best they could
and to descend upon the Gauls from the north.
Hanno effected this manœuver and sent up smoke
signals to advise Hannibal that all was ready.

Thus the Gauls, prepared to demolish the

Carthaginians as they landed, were suddenly set upon from the rear by a terrifying and entirely unexpected force. They quickly dispersed and Hannibal, knowing of Scipio's approach, hurried northward along the east bank of the river and then pressed on toward Italy's last and most stalwart line of defense.

Scipio, discovering that he had been outguessed, returned to Italy and pitched his camp on the river Po, prepared to capture such small remnants of Hannibal's force as might straggle down the southern slopes of the Alps.

There is no definite record of Hannibal's incredible passage of the Alps—no way of telling positively which of seven possible routes he used. Livy, however, gives us an extraordinary picture of this great event, pieced together, probably, from scraps of information furnished to the Romans by Carthaginian prisoners.

Aside from the terrible natural obstacles that he must inevitably have overcome, Hannibal was faced with determined opposition from the native barbarians, who resented this inexplicable intrusion of their mountain fastnesses by dusky men and gargantuan beasts. At one time, when the Carthaginians were proceeding in close formation along a narrow and precarious ledge, the natives effected a surprise attack with rocks and boulders rolled down from above.

The army was thrown into confusion and in the general panic that ensued great numbers were pushed over the edge, and men, horses and elephants, in an awful, struggling mass, rolled down the face of the cliff "like some vast fabric." *

"Despondency had begun to seize the minds of the soldiers. The paths that were becoming ever more difficult, the provisions failing, the marching through defiles exposed to the constant attacks of foes whom they could not reach, the sadly thinned ranks, the hopeless situation of the stragglers and the wounded, the object which appeared chimerical to all save the enthusiastic leader—all these things began to tell even on the African and Spanish veterans. But the confidence of the general remained the same." †

Somehow or other Hannibal managed to hold his discouraged army together; somehow or other he inspired them, and their stumbling horses, and their puzzled elephants, to go on—and fifteen days after he had started the ascent of the Alps he led the Carthaginians down into the pleasant green fields of Italy, where the Cisalpine Gauls were friendly and hospitable and where Rome and final triumph seemed near at hand.

The struggles with the Gauls and the far more terrible struggles with the Alps had left Hannibal with twenty thousand infantry and six thousand

* Livy, Book XXI.   † Mommsen, Book III.

cavalry, many of the latter being without mounts. Unfortunately, we have no statistics on the number of survivors in the elephant brigade, but there can't have been many of them left.

So the Romans, under Scipio, advanced to meet the Carthaginians with high hopes of instant and conclusive victory. The career of this presumptuous young African was to be brought to an end.

Before the battle, there were two evil omens in the Roman camp: a wolf entered the enclosure, bit some of the soldiers, and escaped; a swarm of bees settled on a tree above Scipio's tent. The indicated wrath of the gods was assuaged with sacrifices and prayers, and Scipio delivered a lengthy address to his troops which reads exactly like the inflammatory exhortation of a football coach to his team before the big game.

Referring contemptuously to the Carthaginians, Scipio said, "They are but the resemblances, nay, are rather the shadows of men; being worn out with hunger, cold, dirt and filth, and bruised and enfeebled among stones and rocks. Besides all this, their joints are frost-bitten, their sinews stiffened with the snow, their limbs withered by the frost, their armor battered and shivered, their horses lame and powerless. With such cavalry, with such infantry, you will have to fight: you will not have enemies in reality, but rather their last remains."

At the conclusion of his speech, Scipio expressed one regret: he lamented that, after the battle, the credit for the conquest of Hannibal would be attributed to the Alps, rather than to him.

Armed with such confidence, the Roman army went forth to meet the shattered Carthaginians on the banks of the Ticinus River, and were subjected to quick and decisive defeat. It was the first of a series of amazing victories for Hannibal —victories which were to deprive Rome of its power and prestige, and to threaten its very existence.

Scipio himself was severely wounded and would have died miserably, or been taken prisoner, had he not been rescued under heroic circumstances by his son, Publius Cornelius Scipio * (later Africanus), who was destined to distinguish himself as the foremost adversary of Hannibal, and the decentest, most gallant gentleman in Roman history.

Rome now realized that it had overestimated the destructive powers of its allies, the Alps, and so the consul Sempronius was dispatched with an army to join Scipio and to finish Hannibal before winter set in.

In December the combined forces under Sempronius (Scipio had not yet recovered from his

* Note.—It is this younger Scipio who appears as a character in "The Road to Rome."

wounds) engaged Hannibal's men on the Trebia
River, and again the Romans were completely
routed. Sempronius himself was killed, and Hannibal was left in absolute control of all the north-
ern provinces.

He settled down in Cisalpine Gaul for the winter, gathering recruits, horses, and supplies—
and, incidentally, promoting so much hard feel-
ing that the local inhabitants heaved sighs of re-
lief when, in the following spring, he broke camp
and headed southward toward the doubtfully
eternal city.

He crossed the Apennines and entered the fe-
verish lowlands of Etruria, where disease inflicted
severe losses on his troops. Another Roman
army, under a new consul, Flaminius, went forth
to block the Carthaginian advance, but Hannibal
outmanœuvered them and pushed into the Etru-
rian hill country. He knew that Flaminius would
rush after him, and he also knew that there was
only one road that Flaminius could take.

So Hannibal assembled his force in ambush on
the slopes above Lake Trasimenus, and while the
Romans were passing through the narrow defile
below, descended upon them and slaughtered them.
Flaminius was killed and his army annihilated;
there was now no line of defense between Hannibal
and Rome.

Livy describes in detail the subsequent scenes
of horror and hysteria in Rome. The citizens and

their leaders believed that the city was doomed; even the gods were preparing to desert them, as evidenced by the dreadful portents which followed. For example, an ox ran amuck in the market-place, entered a building, climbed to the third story and plunged to destruction on the pavement below.

Something, obviously, had to be done—first, to conciliate the gods, and second, to organize a practical defense against Hannibal. The latter and more difficult task was assigned to Quintus Fabius Maximus, the venerable politician who had held war and peace in the folds of his robe. He was proclaimed dictator and was given supreme control of the state and its armies.

Fabius was a leading exponent of the old regime in Rome—a cautious, conservative reactionary. To-day, he would be numbered among the stand-patters of the Republican party, and would undoubtedly be high in the favor of the White House Spokesman. Mommsen says of him: "Zealous in his reverence for the good old times, for the political omnipotence of the senate, and for the command of the burgomasters, he looked—next to sacrifices and prayer—to a methodical prosecution of the war as the main means of saving the state." Like so many politicians, before and since, Fabius represented a harmonious and convenient combination of shrewdness and stupidity.

Hannibal failed to follow up his victory at Trasimenus; instead of marching directly to Rome, he chose to cut across Italy, attempting to gain allies so that the isolation of Rome would be complete. The Italian states, however, were cold to Hannibal's proposals, and he was compelled to continue, as best he could, with his ever-diminishing force.

The famous Fabian policy of delay was now in practise, and such forces as Rome could put into the field were instructed to watch Hannibal closely but never, under any circumstances, to risk the chances of actual battle.

In the fall of 217, a year after his passage of the Alps, Hannibal found himself in a precarious position. He was caught in a pocket, surrounded by Romans who commanded the heights; he faced the necessity of wintering "amid the rocks of Forniæ and the sands and hideous swamps of Liternium." *

Hannibal, like Captain Flagg, had to think fast, and he evolved one of those ruses which caused the Romans to complain bitterly that he didn't play fair. Two thousand oxen were assembled, and fagots attached to their horns. At night, these fagots were lighted and the oxen were driven up the slopes held by the legions; of course, the startled oxen stampeded and the Romans, terrified by this astounding demonstration, stam-

* Livy. Book XXI

peded with them. Perhaps they associated this flaming herd with the ox which had committed suicide in Rome, and concluded that the gods were intervening again.

When the stratagem had finally been discovered, Hannibal and his army had passed the Roman lines and were headed for the comfortable plains of Apulia, to the eastward.

Fabius followed, and the two armies settled down for the winter. In the light of modern, long-range warfare, it is interesting to note that, for the next few months, the Romans and Carthaginians were encamped within sight of each other, a few hundred yards apart.

In the meantime, the popularity of Fabius Maximus was on the wane. He had managed to stand Hannibal off, but the Roman people were demanding a victory in loud and insistent tones, and Fabius's timid tactics were subjected to emphatic criticism. Marcus Minucius, master of the horse, persuaded the Senate to place him in a position of authority equal to that of Fabius, and the Roman army confronting Hannibal was thus divided into two camps.

Hannibal promptly provoked Marcus Minucius to action, and administered a severe beating. This finished Marcus Minucius, and Fabius was again restored to full power. (Hannibal must have had an excellent spy system; at all times, he

seems to have been perfectly aware of everything
that went on in Rome.)

Fabius was still unpopular, however, and in the
spring of 216 two new consuls were elected, and
the dictatorship came to an end. One of the
consuls was an insurgent young man named Terrentius Varro—the son of a wealthy butcher, and
looked down upon by the patricians as one of the
nouveau-riche; the other consul was Æmilius
Paullus, a friend of Fabius's and a supporter of
his policies.

Varro and Æmilius were dispatched to the
army in Apulia, taking command on alternate
days. The two men disliked and distrusted each
other: Varro believed in forcing the issue with
Hannibal, whose army was vastly inferior in
numbers; Æmilius believed in proceeding cautiously.

Hannibal retreated, as though fearing to meet
the superior force. On the days when Varro
commanded, the Roman army moved forward rap-
idly; on alternate days, it moved slowly, warily.

It was on one of the Varro days that Hannibal
turned and faced the Romans at Cannæ, on the
Aufidus River. He had approximately fifty thousand men, as against ninety thousand Romans.
Furthermore, his position was a bad one, with
swampy land and the river itself behind him, and
therefore no opportunity for organized retreat
in case of emergency.

He placed his weakest troops—his Spanish and Gallic infantry—in the center of his line, with his heavy African infantry and his superb Numidian cavalry at either wing.

Then he invited Varro to attack, which Varro cheerfully did. The Spaniards and the Gauls gave way, and the Romans swept through Hannibal's lines, believing that they were winning a great victory. When Varro's impetuous men had advanced a sufficient distance, Hannibal sent his African infantry against them from the sides in solid formation. His cavalry wheeled around and attacked them from the rear. Thus, as the result of Hannibal's strategy, the field was completely reversed, and the Romans found themselves floundering about in the swamps and in the bloody waters of the Aufidus.

The number of Romans killed in the battle of Cannæ was close to seventy thousand. Many more were taken prisoner. Æmilius Paullus was killed, as were Marcus Minucius, the former rival of Fabius Maximus, and eighty men of senatorial rank. Terrentius Varro, with seventy horsemen, took refuge in Venusia; the other remnants of the Roman army were assembled, by the younger Scipio, in Canusium.

Rome itself went mad with grief and fear, the horror which followed Trasimenus being increased tenfold after this colossal disaster. Every home

in the city mourned for the "consumed youth of
Cannæ"; * every Roman waited, in agonized ter-
ror, for the appearance of Hannibal at the gates.

Hannibal had reached the culminating point in
his career. He had wiped out one army on the
Ticinus, another on the Trebia and a third at
Lake Trasimenus; now, at Cannæ, he had demolished the last vestiges of Roman power in one
vast, overwhelming victory. The Italian states,
from Capua down, rejoiced at the prospective
collapse of their imperialistic and domineering
neighbor, and flocked to Hannibal's standard.
From Macedon came messages indicating that
King Philip was ready to ally himself with Carthage. Even Carthage itself—ever reluctant to
support Hannibal with reinforcements or supplies
or money—even lazy Carthage appeared to take
an interest in the progress of its expeditionary
force.

Hannibal was supreme. Rome was his oyster;
he could open it and devour it at his leisure.

The night after Cannæ, when the gasps and the
stifled cries of dying men were still to be heard,
the Carthaginian officers clustered about Hannibal and urged him not to wait—to press on to
Rome and to finish the great work of destruction.
But Hannibal shook his head; he told them
that the time for final triumph had not yet come.

* Iuvenal. II. 153.

Perhaps he knew, vaguely, that the time would never come.

It was then that Maharbal, bitterly disappointed, said to Hannibal, "You know how to gain victories, but not how to use them."

Such was the peak in the story of Hannibal's remarkable life. After Cannæ, he started on the down-grade—and his record, thereafter, is one of discouragement and final defeat.

The allegiance of the Italian states availed him nothing, the support promised by Philip of Macedon never arrived and every attempt made to send reinforcements from Carthage or Spain failed. Hannibal's brother, Hasdrubal, led an expedition along the celebrated roads through Gaul and across the Alps, but his army was defeated on the Metaurus. News of this battle was conveyed to Hannibal when the jeering Romans hurled Hasdrubal's head into his brother's camp.

Fabius Maximus again came into power in Rome, the Senate realizing that, in so far as Hannibal was concerned, it was better to be safe than sorry. They reasoned, and with considerable justification, that even though Fabius won no glorious victories, neither did he suffer any crushing defeats. So Hannibal wandered about Italy for thirteen years, in a determined but futile endeavor to revive the waning hopes of his tired little army.

When the Romans had sufficiently recovered from the disaster at Cannæ, new legions were recruited and trained and sent to besiege Capua, as a punishment for the Capuan alliance with Hannibal. In an effort to raise this siege by diverting the Roman forces, Hannibal marched his men to Rome, and camped outside the city.

Here for a few days he "hung with his dusky army, like a storm-cloud about to break, within sight of the sentinels on the walls of Rome." * The cry of "Hannibal at the gates" went up within the city, and there was a new outburst of the hysterical fear that the name of the Carthaginian invader always inspired.

The Romans, peering nervously at their imminent enemies, supposed that Hannibal intended to lay siege to the city. They saw him advance, with his cavalry, and ride slowly around the walls, while the African war drums of the Carthaginian host beat ominously. But he made no attempt to storm those walls; he hurled a javelin against one of the gates of Rome, and rode away.

In 202, fifteen years after his entry into Italy, Hannibal was called home to defend Carthage, which was menaced as a result of the victories won by the younger Scipio in Africa.

Hannibal attempted to negotiate treaties with Scipio—the same Scipio who had seen the Car-

* Frazer's "The Golden Bough."

thaginians overwhelm the Roman legions on the
Ticinus and the Trebia, at Trasimenus and at
Cannæ; these efforts, however, were unavailing,
and the two armies fought it out on the river
Zama.   There, for the first time, Hannibal met
defeat.

Carthage became a tributary state, paying rep-
arations to Rome so enormous that, the Romans
confidently believed, Carthage would never be able
to recover.   Tired of war, tired of the discour-
agements and disillusionments that he had faced
through fifteen lonely years, Hannibal turned to
statesmanship and, as civil leader in Carthage,
proved that his genius was not limited to the pro-
fession of arms.

He organized Carthage on a sound, sensible
basis, and promoted prosperity to such an extent
that Rome again became jealous and nervous.
Not only was Carthage paying its indemnities
promptly; it was actually gaining in wealth and
in power on the side.

The Romans demanded that Hannibal either be
assassinated or surrendered to them, and Scipio
Africanus was instructed to see that this was
done.   Scipio, however, would have no part in a
scheme that was prompted by meanness and
vengeful spite.   He admired Hannibal, and re-
spected him as an officer and a gentleman, and
the contemptible machinations of his countrymen
disgusted him.

In the year 195, Hannibal solved the difficulty by going into voluntary exile. The Romans, however, were still unsatisfied. Hannibal had injured the dignity of Rome by his success; he had made their mighty city look small in the eyes of the world—and he must die. For another thirteen years they hounded him from one haven of refuge to another; his life was constantly in danger, first in Tyre, the mother city of Carthage; then at the court of Antiochus the Great, at Ephesus; then in Crete, to which he had fled when Antiochus was subjected to pressure from Rome, and finally in Bithynia.

In 183, when Hannibal was in Bithynia, the Romans prevailed upon King Prusias to deliver him to them. Prusias, terrified by Roman threats, would have done so, but Hannibal opened a seal ring that he always carried and took from it the poison which ended his life. So Hannibal perished, in inglorious obscurity—a man who had lived a magnificently eventful life, and had lived it utterly in vain. Scipio Africanus, Hannibal's persistent adversary and, ultimately, his friend, died in the same year.

Carthage itself did not long survive its distinguished leader. Rome had changed since the days of Fabius Maximus and the decent Scipios; its government was in the hands of evil, lustful,

vindictive men, like Cato, who gloried in conquest
and bloodshed and destruction. "Delenda est
Carthago!" These terrible words, uttered by
Cato at the conclusion of every speech, have been
dinned into the ears of restless schoolboys from
time immemorial. They formed the death sentence of Carthage.

Cato had visited Carthage, had observed the
magnificence of its temples and the apparent
happiness of its people, and would not rest until
its comfortable prosperity was crushed.

His resentful arguments prevailed, and a Roman army and navy were sent to blockade
Carthage and to starve it into a state of submission. For years the Punic citadel held out—
its people, in their hour of desperation, display-
ing an unprecedented degree of fortitude and gallant determination. The courage that had carried Carthaginians across the Alps, that had
sustained them through fifteen years of warfare
on foreign soil, was evident when Carthage made
its last stand.

In 146 B. C., the city fell. Its buildings and
its monuments were utterly destroyed, and the
wasted remnants of its once huge population were
enslaved. The tragedy of Carthage, and of
Hamilcar and Hannibal, was ended.

Rome ruled the world. Its last and most formidable rival had been obliterated. There was

nothing left to conquer, except the unknown lands
that lay beyond the rim of the horizon. . . .

The stage was set for the dramatic entrance
of Julius Cæsar. The tragedy of Rome was about
to begin.

* * * *

Hannibal's action in turning away from Rome
has always puzzled students of military history.
The Romans explained at great length that he was
frightened away, bluffed away or awed by a portent from the gods; but Napoleon and many others refuse to accept these explanations. They say
that if any frightening, bluffing or awing were
done, it was always Hannibal who did it. Hannibal outwitted the Romans with almost miraculous
consistency for fifteen years, and it is difficult to
believe that a pompous politician like Fabius
Maximus, or even a determined young fighter like
Scipio, could have wheedled him from the main
object of his life's efforts, once he had eliminated
the last obstacles that stood in his way.

Nor is it reasonable to suppose that Hannibal
could have been diverted from his purpose by divine intervention. He was unquestionably far too
intelligent for that.

Why, then, did he march from Cannæ to Capua
instead of to Rome? Why did he refuse to listen
to the impassioned pleas of his officers, who knew

that the opportunity to strike their final, conclusive blow had come?

These questions are unanswerable, and Hannibal remains clouded in an atmosphere of glamor-
ous, romantic mystery. For this reason, he is
calculated to excite the sympathy of the senti-
mental observer and to stimulate his imagination.
That, at least, has been the effect on me since the
time when I started (under compulsion) to study
the confusing history of the First, Second, and
Third Punic Wars.

It seemed possible to me that Hannibal, after
the battle of Cannæ, was suddenly afflicted with
an attack of acute introspection—that he paused
to ask of himself the devastating question, "What
of it?", and that he was unable to find an answer.
In resolving this idea into a three-act play, I
realized that I couldn't express it all in the form
of a soliloquy by Hannibal; there would have to
be a character to put these disturbing thoughts
into Hannibal's mind. As there was no record
that such a character existed at the time I took
it upon myself to invent one in Amytis, the purely
fictitious wife of Fabius Maximus.*

"The Road to Rome," therefore, has its prin-
cipal being in the person of a character who did
not exist. Nor is this its only non-historical

---

* NOTE.—Fabius Maximus did have a wife, but she was not a
Greek, and there is not the slightest chance that her son had any
traces of Phœnician blood.

aspect. Any one who reads through the forego-
ing preface, and through the play itself, will
realize that I have taken more than one liberty
with the actual, or rather, the recorded facts.

I have assumed that Hannibal marched directly
to Rome after the sweeping victory at Cannæ and
that his inexplicable change of heart occurred
while he was encamped before the gates of the
city. I have also suggested that the appoint-
ment of Fabius as dictator was made at this time.

Few members of the audiences have noticed
these flagrant distortions, and it is in an attempt
to do the right thing by history that I publish
this lengthy account of Hannibal's career.

Although "The Road to Rome" does not con-
form religiously to the general outline of history,
I have tried to present its characters—Hannibal,
Hasdrubal, Fabius, and Scipio—with due regard
for the ascertainable truth. The representation
of Rome itself, as it existed under the Republic,
is not unjustifiable, for the spirit of Fabius Maximus and his brother boosters has become the spirit
of America to-day. History is full of deadly and
disturbing parallels and this, it seems to me, is
one of the most obvious parallels of all. Furthermore, I have attempted to make all the people in
the play credible and recognizable—and in doing
so, I have caused a great many dramatic critics
to cry, "Shaw—Shaw—Shaw!"

This critical tendency to mention the eminent Fabian, while supremely flattering in one respect, has afforded me considerable pain. The use of modern colloquialisms in classical dress does not, in my opinion, indicate a deliberate imitation of George Bernard Shaw any more than the introduction of a seduction scene would necessarily indicate an imitation of Elinor Glyn.

The conversation of the Roman citizens in "Julius Cæsar," and of the Greeks in "Timon of Athens," proved that Shakespeare was not reluctant to put current Elizabethan wheezes into the mouths of the ancients. Subsequently, however, the Shakespeare tradition became so heavy in the drama that writers of historical plays have considered it a matter of duty to be ponderously Elizabethan in style; all historical characters on the stage have conversed in blank verse, employing phrases like "How now, sirrah!", which, in point of fact, are as thoroughly non-classical as "What's the big idea?"

In reviewing one of Rostand's less conspicuous dramas, Shaw wrote, "If Melissinde would only eat something, or speak in prose, or only swear in it, or do anything human—were it even smoking a cigarette"—and thereby gave utterance to a complaint that had bothered less articulate people for years. In this respect, I, among others, have followed Shaw's excellent advice. In all other respects, there is not the slightest reason to associate "The Road to Rome" with "Cæsar and Cleopatra," as Shaw himself would be the first to concede, loudly.

"The Road to Rome" was inspired by an unashamedly juvenile hero-worship for Hannibal; in manner and in intent, it is incorrigibly romantic. No author with Shavian pretensions could conceivably start building on a basis like that.

Whether or not Mr. Shaw started it, there is now a widespread and generally commendable conspiracy to divest history of its text-book formality, and to present historic personages with the same easy intimacy that is displayed by Texas Guinan when introducing a new Black Bottom dancer.

Clio has always been an austere figure, clad in marble robes and perched up before public libraries for the purpose of scaring away those who approach such dignified edifices with other than a serious, studious intent. Nowadays, Clio is being urged to step down from her pedestal and meet the boys.

Wells incurred the wrath of the literal-minded when he dared to question the traditional greatness of Alexander, Cato, and Cæsar, among others. The same tendency is evident in innumerable recent biographies—by Gamaliel Bradford, Lytton Strachey, Philip Guedalla, W. E. Woodward,

Emil Ludwig, and almost any one else who can find a suitable subject for exposition. It is obviously evident, too, in such books as Paul de Kruif's "Microbe Hunters" and Will Durant's "The Story of Philosophy," and in John Erskine's interpretations of Homeric and Arthurian legends.

The popular taste for such historical revelations is attributable, I feel sure, to the enormous appetite for "true confessions" and "success stories" in the more widely circulated magazines. Just as the romantic rise of Frank A. Munsey from newsboy to millionaire publisher provides fascinating reading, so does that of Napoleon Bonaparte from friendless recruit to world conqueror; the good, substantial citizen who wants to know what Pola Negri does in her own time has lately become equally curious as to the private life of Helen of Troy.

People are beginning to realize that history is actually the biography of mankind and, as such, the greatest "success story" that has ever been written. What could be more dramatic, more inspirational, than the narrative of man's ascent from an impoverished, illiterate cave-dweller to a Calvin Coolidge or a Henry L. Mencken?

"The Road to Rome" is, of course, another evidence of this undeniable trend—another offspring of the union between fiction and fact. In presenting historic events and people in terms of modern life, I am using a formula that is not new; the fact that it is not new, however, does not signify that it is illegitimate.

One critic, in reviewing "The Road to Rome," complained that I have introduced all the cliches of humorous journalism with which, as a result of my association with *Life*, I am unhappily familiar. There is, in the play, a neglected wife, who spends too much money on clothes and wants to go out to the movies; there is an unimaginative, unappreciative tired-business-man of a husband who doesn't understand; there is even a bossy, envious mother-in-law who coddles her darling son and abominates his restless wife.

These elementary characters and characteristics are used deliberately, in the first act, to establish, as expeditiously as possible, an atmosphere with which an audience will be familiar. Deliberate, also, is the use of "What Price Glory?" terms, and the suggestion of a "What Price Glory?" attitude, in the Carthaginian Expeditionary Force. The guardsmen who appear in "The Road to Rome" are professional soldiers —weary, fed-up, and interested only in the opportunities for booty which their victories may offer. It sounds incongruous for one of Hannibal's soldiers to say, "I don't do no turn with no elephants, see?" It would sound still more incongruous, I stoutly maintain, if he were to express himself in lusty Elizabethan or even in perfect Oxonian English.

The weight of the Shakespearian tradition on historical dramas, and of the Walter Scott tradition on historical novels, has impelled writers with a regard for a naturalistic style to avoid historical subjects. The ruthless shattering of these traditions that is now going on may be carried to ridiculous extremes—in "The Road to Rome" and elsewhere—but the spirit that inspires it is none the less laudable because of that. There's no earthly reason why history should continue to be chastely academic and formidably dull.

* * *

A preface to a play cannot be strictly legal without some mention of the author's debt of gratitude to those who have brought his manuscript to life on the stage. Any one who has seen "The Road to Rome," as played by Jane Cowl, will realize that my own debt of gratitude is exceptionally large.

To Miss Cowl, then, for the loveliness and graciousness, the gaiety and tenderness, that she has given to the character of Amytis; to Philip Merivale, for his fine, sturdy, and sympathetic impersonation of Hannibal; to all the others in an excellent and thoroughly pleasant cast; to Lester Lonergan, for his sensitive and intelligent direction; to Lee Simonson, for the gorgeousness and the complete rightness of the settings and costumes; to the Messrs. Brady and Wiman, for providing such a handsome and ample production, and to the critics (I refer only to those of them who gave the play unqualified praise), I murmur a fervent "Thank you," and with that expression of profound appreciation this long-winded preface is brought gratefully to a close.   R. E. S.

February, 1927.

THE ROAD TO ROME

THE ROAD TO ROME

Presented by Messrs. William A. Brady, Jr., and Dwight Deere Wiman at the Belasco Theatre, Washington, D. C., January 17th, 1927; the Broad Street Theatre, Newark, N. J., January 24th, and the Playhouse, New York, January 31st, with the following cast:

VARIUS	Mr. Fairfax Burgher
META	Miss Joyce Carey
FABIA	Miss Jessie Ralph
FABIUS MAXIMUS	Mr. Richie Ling
AMYTIS	Miss Jane Cowl
TANUS	Mr. Peter Meade
CATO	Mr. William Pearce
SCIPIO	Mr. Charles Brokaw
DRUSUS	Mr. William R. Randall
SERTORIUS	Mr. Lionel Hogarth
TIBULLUS	Mr. Alfred Webster
SERGEANT	Mr. Jock McGraw
CORPORAL	Mr. Lewis Martin
FIRST GUARDSMAN	Mr. Clement O'Loghlen
SECOND GUARDSMAN	Mr. Ben Lackland
THIRD GUARDSMAN	Mr. Walter A. Kinsella
FOURTH GUARDSMAN	Mr. John McNulty
FIFTH GUARDSMAN	Mr. Willard Joray
THOTHMES	Mr. Lionel Hogarth
HASDRUBAL	Mr. Louis Hector
MAHARBAL	Mr. Alfred Webster
CARTHALO	Mr. Harold Moffet
MAGO	Mr. Barry Jones
HANNIBAL	Mr. Philip Merivale
BALA	Mr. Gert Pouncy

Staged by Mr. Lester Lonergan
Costumes and settings designed by Mr. Lee Simonson

SCENES

ACT I.—*Courtyard in the home of* FABIUS MAXIMUS *in Rome*: a June evening in the year 216 B. C.

ACT II.—HANNIBAL'S *headquarters in a temple, about a mile east of Rome*; an hour later.

ACT III.—*The same as Act II ;* the next morning.

ACT I

THE ROAD TO ROME

ACT I

The curtain rises, disclosing a scene in the courtyard, or atrium, in the home of FABIUS MAXIMUS *in Rome. It is early evening, just before sunset, of a June day in the year 216 B. C.*

The house, which surrounds the courtyard on all three sides, is one story in height. It is simple and unostentatious in design, being representative of Rome in the period of the Republic, when the sterner virtues of economy and almost Spartan frugality were practised.

There are four entrances: one (downstage right) which leads to the kitchens and slave quarters; another (upstage right) which leads to the street—this being the main entrance to the house; a third (downstage left) which leads to the sleeping quarters, and a fourth (upstage left) which leads, through a passageway, to the street.

The scene is divided in half, laterally, by a row of columns. Over the front part of the stage is stretched a painted awning, or peplum; behind the columns, the atrium is open, the blue Italian sky being visible above the rear wall of the house.

7

In this open space is a small pool; flowers and shrubs are growing in earthenware pots; there is a shrine in a niche in the rear wall.

At the right, in the foreground, is a table, with three chairs and a stool. Behind it, against the columns, is a sort of serving-table on which are goblets, bowls, pitchers, etc. At the left is another chair and a bench.

When the curtain rises, VARIUS, *a slave, is engaged in setting the table for the evening meal. He is a fair young man, obviously not a Latin, with the air of one who has known better circumstances than these. He is supremely contemptuous of his Roman masters, and inclined to be rebellious.*

VARIUS *pours some wine into a goblet, peers about cautiously to make sure that he is unobserved, and then tastes the wine.*

VARIUS *(calling off to the right)*

This wine is terrible. Haven't we anything better in the house?

META *(off stage)*

No. That's all we have. (META, *a slim, lovely young girl, enters, bearing a bowl of grapes which she deposits on the table.*) And there's none too much of that!

VARIUS

I wish they'd hurry up and settle this war so that we could have something decent to eat and drink.

META

It's not for a slave to criticize his master's wine.

VARIUS (*sitting down at the table*)

Oh, I know it—but I'm fed up with keeping my place. (*He stands up, hastily.*)

META

Perhaps I'm fed up, too, Varius. Being a slave in Rome isn't quite the pleasantest occupation imaginable. . . . But I should like to know what's to be done about it.

VARIUS

Slaves sometimes escape.

META (*alarmed*)

Don't speak of that again, Varius. You mustn't dare to try that. You know what the chances are. If you were caught, it would mean instant death!

VARIUS

Wouldn't you prefer death to this?

META

No—I can't say that I would.

Varius

You're better off than I am. You're close to her. She gives you some sympathy. She understands.

Meta

She understands us because she's an alien herself.

Varius

Yes, and in Rome the attitude toward all aliens is, "If you don't like it here, why don't you go back where you came from"—knowing damned well that we can't.

Meta

Cheer up, Varius. (*She puts her arm about him and strokes his hair.*) It might have been worse—it might have been much worse. Suppose we had been separated when they captured us?

Varius

I know. But why can't we have our love? Why are we compelled to smother our natural impulses? We belong to each other—but we can't have each other, because we're slaves!

Meta

In Rome, it's wise for a slave to forget that he is a human being.

Varius

If you weren't here, I might be able to forget

it. (*He takes her in his arms.*) But when I look at you, I can't remember anything—except that I love you.

META

And I love you, Varius. I shall always love you. (*She backs away from him, nervously.*)

VARIUS (*vehemently*)

We must escape, Meta! We must get away from Rome, and be free!

META

We can't get away from Rome, Varius. Rome is everywhere. Rome will soon be the whole world.

VARIUS

If we could only reach Apulia, we could join with the Carthaginians.

META

Even that's hopeless. The Roman army has cornered them at last. I heard the master say that he expected news of Hannibal's defeat any day.

VARIUS

The master doesn't always know what he's talking about.

META

Of course he doesn't know what he's talking about. He's not supposed to. He's a Senator. . . . But I couldn't go and leave her. She needs us, Varius. She's bored to death in Rome. . . .

VARIUS

She can't be blamed for that.

META

We're her only friends. She clings to us.

VARIUS (*excitedly*)

Perhaps she'd escape with us!

META

If she knew of any way of escape from Rome, she would have taken it herself, long ago. . . . Now please put the thought out of your mind, Varius. We can't escape—ever.

VARIUS

There must be some way out for us.
(*She kisses him tenderly.*)

(FABIA *comes in suddenly from the sleeping-quarters at the left, and gasps, with horrified indignation, at the sight of the two slaves embraced.* FABIA *is the mother of* FABIUS—*a cross, narrow-minded old lady, whose world is her home. For all her seventy-three years, she is brisk and vigorous, and she rules the establishment with an iron hand.*)

FABIA (*astounded at this breach*)

What on earth do you two think you're doing? (*Hastily they separate, with sheepish self-consciousness.*) Why, I never heard of such loose, shocking behavior—never in all my life. How dare you kiss each other—right here in the atrium, of all places? I don't look for much delicacy among slaves, but you know as well as I do that this sort of thing is forbidden. You'll be punished for this.

META (*abjectly*)

We're very sorry that it happened, my lady.

FABIA

I declare, you slaves are becoming more insolent every day. You're a problem, that's what you are. How dare you insult your master's house with such conduct?

VARIUS

We were making love to each other, my lady. It's an old custom in our country.

FABIA

Oh, it is, is it? Well, you're not in your country now. You're in Rome! Furthermore, you're slaves. If the people in your country had spent less time making *love*, and more at good, honest, hard work, perhaps our Roman armies wouldn't have conquered you so easily.

META

Yes, my lady.

FABIA

Is dinner ready?

Meta

It is, my lady.

Fabia

See that it's nicely served. (*The bolt on the outer door is heard.*) And I don't care to hear of any more *love*-making in this house. Do you understand?

Varius

We do, my lady—perfectly.

(Fabius *enters from the right—the street entrance.*)

Meta (*to* Varius)

The master!

(*Fabius is a typical Senator—pompous, unctuous, consciously important and 100 per cent Roman. His most casual utterance is delivered, as it were, from the eminence of the rostrum. He is not, however, just an old wind-bag—inflated, for purposes of this play, merely to be punctured. On the contrary, he should convey a definite sense of authority, distinction and real power. He is, at the moment, at the head of the Roman state; he must "fit the picture-frame."*)

Fabia

Ah, my poor son! (*She anxiously scans his face.*) You look tired.

Fabius

Yes, mother. I've had a hard day at the

forum. (*He sinks down on the bench at the left.*
META *goes out at the right.*) These are trying
times, mother, trying times. Rome faces a grave
crisis.

FABIA

What is the crisis now, my son?

FABIUS

The people are worried about Hannibal. He
has the most irritating habit of winning victories,
and our generals have been unable to check his
advance. There is a demand in the Senate for
positive action.

FABIA

Oh, don't listen to these old senators. They're
always talking. Talk—talk—talk! That's all
they know how to do.

FABIUS

To-day the Senator really accomplished something, mother—something big. They took con-
structive, intelligent measures to combat the
Carthaginian menace.

FABIA

What did they do?
(META *enters quietly from the right, carrying
a pitcher of water.*)

FABIUS

I am proud to say that they recognized your

son's long and not undistinguished career as a public servant of Rome.

FABIA (*excitedly*)

They promoted you?

FABIUS (*rising*)

They proclaimed me Dictator, with full power to conduct the state and the armies as I see fit.

FABIA

My boy! The Dictator of all Rome. (*She smothers him with congratulatory caresses.*) You have brought new glory to the Fabian name. You are the greatest man in the world. (*She turns to the slaves.*) Here, you slaves! Do you realize the honor that has come to our house? Your master is dictator of all Rome. (*The two slaves bow politely.*)

FABIUS (*deprecatingly*)

Oh, come, come, mother. I'm afraid it isn't quite so much as all that. Just a war-time measure, for purposes of—of expediency.

FABIA

Ah—but you are modest. You begrudge yourself the satisfaction of knowing that all Rome must bow before you now. (*She contemplates the possibilities.*) When I walk out into the streets of the city, everyone—even the best families—will bow before *me*, and say, "She is the mother of Fabius Maximus, the Dictator of all Rome!"

FABIUS

My dear, loyal mother. (*He pats her hand patronizingly.*) I'm rather anxious to see how Amytis takes this bit of news.

(FABIA's *brow clouds.*)

FABIA

Oh, she'll be delighted, of course.

FABIUS

I hurried home from the Forum to tell her about it. Where is she?

FABIA

She should have been here long ago. It is past the hour of dinner.

FABIUS

Meta, where is your mistress?

META

She has been down at the market-place.

FABIUS (*rising*)

At the market-place? What for?

META

There is a merchant there, lately arrived from Antioch.

Fabius

From Antioch, eh? What business has he in Rome?

Varius

I think he came here in the hope that he might make some money.

Fabius

Or perhaps to pick up some valuable information. Antioch and Carthage are close allies. He may even be spreading Carthaginian propaganda. . . . I'll run the fellow out of town.

Fabia

You can do it, Fabius. *You're* the dictator!

(Fabius *goes over to the table and dips his fingers in the bowl of water which* Meta *holds out to him, drying them with the towel which she also offers.*)

Fabius

It doesn't look well for my wife to be patronizing a dirty foreign peddler. I wish she'd come home.

Fabia

Perhaps we'd better start dinner and not wait for her.

(Fabius *and* Fabia *sit down at the table and start eating.* Varius *goes out.* Fabia *leans over to speak to* Fabius, *confidentially.*

FABIA

I'm very much worried about those slaves. They're becoming more and more insolent all the time.

FABIUS

In what way?

FABIA

Just now, I caught them making love . . .

FABIUS

Making *love?*

FABIA

They were *kissing* each other!

(META, *realizing that she is not supposed to overhear this conversation, tactfully goes out.*)

FABIUS

I hope you spoke to them about it.

FABIA

I reprimanded them—but not so severely as I should. It isn't entirely their fault.

FABIUS

Why not? (*The door bolt is heard again.*)

FABIA

Because they're continually being encouraged to violate the rules of discipline.

FABIUS

By whom?

(AMYTIS *enters from the right, upstage. She is followed by* TANUS, *a slave, who carries garments and materials of brilliant colors.*)

FABIA (*with a gesture toward* AMYTIS)

By her!

(AMYTIS *is young, beautiful, gracious, and obviously civilized. She has an air of culture, sophistication, and refinement that is not evident in any of the Romans. Her mother was an Athenian Greek—her father a Roman officer—and within her are combined the worthiest characteristics of these two widely contrasted races: superficially, she is frivolous, frothy, apparently oblivious of the more serious problems with which her distinguished husband is continally wrestling; but behind this surface artificiality are profound depths of sympathy and understanding. Her external fluffiness and levity are masks for an essential thoughtfulness. She gives the impression, to* FABIUS *and his friends, that she is weak and inconsequential; actually, she is strong, and brave and wise.*)

AMYTIS (*talking rather fast*)

I'm so sorry to be late, but there was a merchant from Antioch who had the most *fascinating* things, and I couldn't tear myself away.

(META *takes* AMYTIS' *cloak, and carries it out at the left, returning presently.*)

FABIA

Amytis, your husband has some great news for you.

AMYTIS (*not having heard*)

Look at this. (*She takes a fragile garment from the slave's arms.*) It's a Phœnician night-gown, from the Court of Antiochus the Great. The merchant told me that it was made for the emperor's favorite concubine.

FABIUS

Amytis! There are servants present.

AMYTIS

And this piece of material. Isn't it gorgeous? Isn't it ravishing? See how it shimmers when you hold it to the light. No Roman loom could have woven fabric like that!

FABIA (*to* FABIUS)

Tell her what happened at the Senate. . . .

AMYTIS (*going right ahead*)

I don't know how I'll use it just yet, but it's bound to come in handy some time or other.

FABIUS

Amytis, the Roman Senate conferred a singular honor on your husband to-day. . . .

AMYTIS (*taking another garment from the slave*)

But here's the real prize—a peacock-green dress from Damascus—made of silk. Think of it! Real silk! The merchant told me that it came from the farthest reaches of the Orient. It was carried on the backs of camels across the desert—"all for you, fair lady"—those were his very words. . . . Isn't it beautiful!

FABIUS

Yes, I suppose so. But do you think—do you think it's quite the sort of thing to be worn by a lady of your position?

AMYTIS

My position? I have no position. I'm just the wife of an ordinary Roman Senator—and, certainly, that doesn't mean much.

FABIA (*bristling*)

The wife of an ordinary Roman Senator, indeed! Do you realize what happened in the Senate to-day?

AMYTIS

Now, *don't* tell me they passed another law.

FABIA

To-day the Roman Senate proclaimed your husband, Fabius Maximus, Dictator.

FABIUS

Yes, my dear, they have placed me at the head of the Roman state.

AMYTIS

Isn't that nice. . . . Tanus, put those things in my room. Go on with dinner. I'll be right back. (*She goes out at the left, with hurried instructions to* TANUS *to "lay them out on the bed so that I can see them all at once."* META *follows her out.*)

FABIUS

She took it calmly.

FABIA (*bitterly*)

She doesn't understand what it means. After all, she's only a Greek.

(FABIUS *resumes his meal.*)

FABIUS

You mustn't be too hard on Amytis, mother. She has those queer Athenian ideas inbred in her, and she can't get rid of them. It isn't her fault. . . . The Athenians know nothing of the principles of government that have made Rome what it is to-day.

FABIA

Yes—and look at Athens now. (META *re-enters.*)

FABIUS (*between mouthfuls*)

Completely gone to seed. No state can survive unless it is founded on good, sound military strength and a policy of progressive conquest.

FABIA

Have we conquered Hannibal yet?

FABIUS

No, we haven't exactly conquered Hannibal as yet.   But he's on the run.

FABIA

All Rome looks to you, my son.

(AMYTIS *comes in and goes to the table.*)

FABIUS

I hope that I shall not be undeserving of my countrymen's trust.

AMYTIS

Well—what have you two been talking about? (*As she speaks, she dips her fingers in the bowl which* VARIUS *holds.*)

FABIA

We've been talking about Hannibal.

FABIUS

I was just telling my mother that we have him on the run.

AMYTIS (*sitting down at the table*)

Everyone seems to be talking about Hannibal these days, and I'm sick and tired of the sound of his name. . . . By the way, who is he?

(FABIUS *and* FABIA *are astounded at this confession of ignorance.*)

FABIUS

My dear Amytis—you're not serious!

AMYTIS

Why not? How should I know who Hannibal is? I'm not a member of the Senate.

FABIUS

Amytis—Hannibal is the arch-enemy of Rome, the invader of Italy. He has threatened the very sanctity of our homes.

AMYTIS

Where does he come from?

FABIUS

From Carthage.

AMYTIS

Really. I've heard that Carthage is a very beautiful city.

FABIUS

Quite possibly. But Carthage happens to be at war with Rome, and Hannibal is in command . . .

AMYTIS

Now, please don't ask me to keep track of our wars, or just who our enemies happen to be at the moment. With one war after another—and sometimes two or three wars at a time—I can't follow them. The mental effort is too great.

FABIUS

Perhaps you'd take a more lively interest if Hannibal marched into Rome, with his army of Africans and Spaniards and Gauls. How would you like to see this house burned down about you,

and your loved ones slaughtered before your eyes?
Would that amuse you?

AMYTIS

It might serve to break the monotony of life in
Rome.

FABIA

I have lived in Rome for seventy-three years.
I have not found it monotonous.

AMYTIS

But, my dear mother, you must remember that
you've never been anywhere else. I had the misfortune to be born in Athens, where gaiety is not
listed among the unpardonable sins.

FABIA

It was bad luck for you that your mother married a Roman officer.

FABIUS

Sometimes I wish that you had inherited more
of your father's traits.

AMYTIS

Perhaps I did. Perhaps my Athenian friv-
olousness is purely superficial. Perhaps, in the
depths of my soul, I am a stern, relentless, world-
beating Roman!

FABIUS

I'm afraid I know nothing about the depths of
your soul, Amytis.

AMYTIS

I'm afraid you don't.

FABIUS

You'll never believe that I am in sympathy with you.

AMYTIS

The trouble with me is—I'm bored. And I don't like it. Being bored is so—so snobbish.

FABIA

It is your own fault if you are bored. There are many subjects of interest in Rome.

FABIUS

My mother is right, Amytis. Rome to-day is the liveliest, most progressive city in the world. Why, just consider the population figures. Ten years ago . . .

AMYTIS

That's just it. Rome is too busily engaged in the great work of expanding to think about such trivial matters as happiness or even contentment. If we could only stop being successful for a change—if we could only *lose* a war, now and then, just for the sake of variety . . .

FABIUS

Our community life is well organized. Why don't you associate with the wives of my friends?

AMYTIS

Now, really, Fabius, you know that Senators themselves are dull; you ought to know that, having to listen to them make speeches all day. But even Senators are marvels of intellectual brilliance compared to their wives.

FABIA (*with obvious scorn*)

I've noticed that you don't care to associate with ladies of the better class.   You seem to prefer the companionship of *slaves*.

FABIUS

Please, mother.   We needn't mention that.

AMYTIS

Fabius . . .

FABIUS

What is it, my dear?

AMYTIS

Couldn't we go out somewhere this evening?

FABIUS

Go *out?*   Where?

AMYTIS

Oh, just somewhere.   To a play, perhaps . . .

FABIA

I see no occasion for going to a play.

FABIUS

Is there a play?

AMYTIS

I believe there is.   There's a company of players here; they come from Athens . . .

FABIUS

Oh!   I've heard about *them*.

AMYTIS

They're giving "Œdipus Rex."

FABIUS (*incredulously*)

And you want to see "Œdipus Rex"?

FABIA

Probably one of the coarsest plays ever written!

AMYTIS

Oh, but I *love* it! I adore a good, exciting tragedy.

FABIUS

But why?

AMYTIS

I love to cry. I like to go into the theatre and just sob.

FABIA (*horrified*)

But "Œdipus Rex" . . .

AMYTIS

What's wrong with that?

FABIUS

To tell you the truth, Amytis. I've never seen the play—but I've heard that it's—well, that it's rather questionable.

AMYTIS

You can't very well judge as to that until you've seen it yourself.

FABIUS

I'm afraid I can't go out again, my dear.

FABIA

Of course you can't, my poor boy. You're terribly tired.

AMYTIS

Then please let me go, anyway.

FABIA

Alone?

Amytis

Why not?

Fabius (*hastily*)

That wouldn't do at all, my dear. I could never consent to that.

Amytis

Then what shall we do this evening—just sit around?

Fabius

No. I shall not just "sit around." I am worn out. I shall go to bed presently.

Amytis

That will be fun.

Fabia

You can clear the table, Varius. (Varius *and* Meta *remove the remains of the meal.*)

Amytis

Is dinner over? (Fabius *rises.*)

Fabia (*belligerently*)

Did you expect anything more?

Amytis (*vaguely*)

I didn't know . . .

Fabia

Of course you didn't know. How could you know? You never take the trouble to *order* the meals.

Amytis

I'm no good at housekeeping.

FABIUS (*with characteristic diplomacy*)

There's no reason why Amytis should attend to the housekeeping, mother—not while you do it so well.

FABIA (*with elaborate scorn*)

Oh, I wouldn't expect her to do any *work* around the house. Oh, no! But it isn't for her to complain.

AMYTIS

I only wanted something sweet. There doesn't seem to be any dessert.

FABIA

Here! Eat a grape. (*She thrusts the bowl of grapes toward* AMYTIS, *who bites one and makes a wry face.*)

AMYTIS

Ugh! Those grapes are sour. (*She motions them away with an expression of disgust.*)

FABIUS

You don't realize that this is war-time, my dear. We have to deny ourselves some of the luxuries, for the sake of our brave boys at the front.

AMYTIS

Is that why there's no dessert?

FABIUS

Yes. This is sweetless Saturday.

(*The meal is now over. The two slaves have cleared the table and gone out, followed by* FABIA, *who superintends their activities. When* FABIUS *and* AMYTIS *are alone,* FABIUS *paces up and down*

*for a few moments, as though trying to find an
opening for an embarrassing subject.*)

FABIUS

It is always difficult for me to talk to you,
Amytis. Sometimes I feel that you and I don't
speak the same language.

AMYTIS

Are you angry with me because I spent so much
money in the market-place?

FABIUS

No—it isn't that—although, I must say, that
Phœnician nightgown seems a little—perhaps——

AMYTIS

Indecent? What of it? None of the Senators
will see me in that, will they? I bought that in
the hope that it might be just the least bit stimu-
lating to you.

FABIUS

And then that green dress—the one that the
camels carried—do you intend to wear that in the
streets of Rome?

AMYTIS

Of course. It will make all the women in Rome
envious, and cause them to complain to their hus-
bands that the wife of Fabius Maximus is not
quite respectable.

FABIUS

But that's what we must avoid. We can't afford to have that sort of talk going on. Don't

forget that you are now the first citizeness of
Rome.

AMYTIS

And therefore the arbiter of fashion, the leader
of thought, the ultimate authority in all matters
relating to feminine deportment.

FABIUS

Of course, of course. You are the dictator's
wife—and for that very reason, you are expected
to set a good example in all the more desirable
virtues.

AMYTIS

Such as?

FABIUS

Well—ah—respectability, modesty, economy,
devotion to duty, reverence, chastity, and—
and . . .

AMYTIS

Mediocrity! I see.

FABIUS

It is in the best interests of the state as a whole.
Do you understand?

AMYTIS

I understand perfectly, and I shall do my best
to be a model of all that is most virtuous and most
thoroughly uninteresting.

FABIUS

And there is one other thing, Amytis.

AMYTIS

I suppose I am to be more regular in my attendance at the temple.

FABIUS

That goes without saying. What I wished particularly was to influence you to take a more lively interest in public affairs. For instance, I was shocked to learn that you know nothing of Hannibal.

AMYTIS

Why should I know anything about Hannibal? Remember, you confessed to me the other day that you had never heard of Aristotle.

FABIUS

That's quite true, my dear. But, after all, you must admit that Aristotle never did anything to make himself famous.

AMYTIS

What has Hannibal done? Has he contributed anything to the advancement of science or philosophy or art?

FABIUS

I'm afraid not. But he has led an army of foot-soldiers, cavalry, and elephants from Africa to Spain, from Spain to Gaul, across the Alps and into Italy—a distance of over three thousand miles. Hannibal is cruel, he is treacherous, he is a menace to our Roman civilization, but he is a great soldier. We must be generous with him and concede him that much.

AMYTIS

You say he is cruel. Is there any soldier who is otherwise?

FABIUS

Hannibal has spread destruction wherever he has gone. His army has burned homes, destroyed crops, butchered men, and despoiled women.

AMYTIS

That is the immemorial privilege of the conqueror . . .

FABIUS

Hannibal has taken undue advantage of that privilege. Last winter, when his army was quartered in Cis-Alpine Gaul, there was a veritable epidemic of pregnancy.

AMYTIS

Good for Hannibal! He sounds like a thoroughly commendable person.

FABIUS

Amytis! Please don't say such things, even in fun.

AMYTIS

Why not? Is it wrong for me to admire good, old-fashioned virility in men? I certainly haven't seen any too much of it in my own life.

FABIUS (*falteringly*)

What do you mean?

AMYTIS

You know perfectly well what I mean, Fabius. . . . Has there been any epidemic of pregnancy around here?

FABIUS

I wish you wouldn't harp on that subject, Amytis. You know that I've been working hard lately. I've had so many worries. It's the state that demands all my time—all my energy . . .

AMYTIS

Of course—the state! What else is there in life but the state, and the state's business, and the state's public brawls . . .

FABIUS

We can have no other thought until Rome rules the world.

AMYTIS

When that happens, I suppose the orgies will start.

FABIUS

The splendid morale of the Roman people will never weaken.

AMYTIS

Morale—there's no such thing in Rome. There's nothing here but a narrow-minded, hypocritical morality. You Romans call it godliness; it's nothing but worldliness, of the most selfish, material kind.

FABIUS

Amytis! I can't bear to hear you talk that way. It—it's cruel.

AMYTIS

Oh—I'm sorry, Fabius. I don't mean to hurt you. Don't pay any attention to the things I say. My ideas don't fit in Rome, anyway. . . . (*She strokes his hair. He is easily mollified.*) Now! Go ahead and tell me all about your success in the Senate, and whatever it was they made you today.

FABIUS (*expanding*)

Dictator. They proclaimed me Dictator of All Rome. I control everything.

AMYTIS

Everything except Hannibal.

FABIUS

I'll have him under control before long. His head will be mounted on a spear in the center of the market-place, as a warning to all those who lack faith in the glorious destiny of Rome.

(AMYTIS *is sitting on the edge of the table and* FABIUS *on the stool before it. Toward the end of the preceding speech,* FABIUS, *warming to his subject, starts to rise with finger pointed upward in a characteristically oratorical gesture.* AMYTIS *places her hands on his shoulders and gently pushes him down again, murmuring, "now, Fabius, please sit down.")*

AMYTIS

All the hopes—all the aspirations of Rome are centered in you—aren't they, Fabius?

FABIUS

Yes, the gods of Rome have called upon me to conquer this ruthless African invader, who has trampled our virgin soil under the dread heel of oppression. (*Again* FABIUS *starts to rise, and again* AMYTIS *restores him to his seat.*)

AMYTIS

Splendid!   Did you use that line in your speech of acceptance?

FABIUS

Yes, I believe I did voice some such sentiments.

AMYTIS

And the Forum rocked with applause, I'm sure.

FABIUS

I'm happy to say that my remarks were well received.   After I had spoken, all the leaders of the Senate clustered around to congratulate me. . . . Would you like to know what else I said?

AMYTIS

Of course I should.

FABIUS (*standing up and achieving an attitude*)

I said: "Fellow Romans, the hour approaches . . ." (*For the third time,* AMYTIS *pushes him back to the stool, saying,* "*Now please, darling— you mustn't get so excited.*")

FABIUS

I pointed with pride to our policy of delay, which has worried Hannibal and forced him to take up a defensive position in Apulia, two hundred miles from Rome. We have caught him in a trap. The army, under the command of Paullus and Varro, confronts the Carthaginians, and is ready to attack. Hannibal's mob is disorganized. His original force has melted to almost nothing, and he has bolstered it up with mutinous, unseasoned barbarians recruited in Spain and Gaul. (*He rises.*) Furthermore, our army outnumbers his by two to one. Our discipline is better, our equipment is better, our morale is better!

AMYTIS

I can just hear the cheers.

FABIUS

The time has come for us to strike—and to strike *hard!*

AMYTIS

Poor Hannibal! After travelling three thousand miles, he has to die ingloriously and be exhibited in the market-place as a horrible lesson to little children.

FABIUS

Waste no sympathy on Hannibal, my dear. He courted disaster when he embarked on this foolhardy enterprise.

AMYTIS

Why do you suppose he did it?

FABIUS

For obvious reasons: he wished to obliterate Rome.

AMYTIS

But why? What has Hannibal against Rome?

FABIUS

He's afraid of us. He knows that unless he destroys Rome first, Rome will ultimately destroy Carthage.

AMYTIS

That seems rather silly.

FABIUS

It may seem silly to you, my dear. The feminine mind can never comprehend the true significance of war.

AMYTIS

Other women do. Whenever one of our armies start out, all the wives and mothers and sweethearts cheer themselves hoarse. And while the men are away, fighting battles and spreading Roman civilization with the sword, the womenfolk sit at home and talk about the great sacrifices they're making. I've heard them. (*She sits down in a chair beside the table.*)

FABIUS

I'm happy to say that the women of Rome have always rallied splendidly in the hour of peril—and I mean no offense to you, my dear. You just don't understand what war is.

AMYTIS

Fabius . . .

FABIUS

Yes?

AMYTIS

How old is Hannibal?

FABIUS

He's just a young man—thirty years of age,
or thereabouts.

AMYTIS

How tragic!

FABIUS

Why tragic?

AMYTIS

I was thinking how wasteful it is to sacrifice a
young man who has the genius to lead a troop of
elephants across the Alps. Just think—if he
were allowed to live, some day he might do something useful.

FABIUS

If he were allowed to live, Amytis, he might
some day cause the downfall of Rome.

AMYTIS

And so you, my husband, are to be celebrated
throughout all history as the man who conquered
Hannibal and saved Rome.

FABIUS (*greatly pleased*)

Yes, my dear—I suppose I shall be accorded
some measure of recognition.

(*There is a slight pause, during which* AMYTIS
gazes off dreamily into space.)

FABIUS

What are you thinking about now, my dear?

AMYTIS

I was just wondering what it would be like to be despoiled.

FABIUS

Amytis! Is that a proper subject for a lady's thoughts?

AMYTIS

Not proper, perhaps—but certainly not unusual.

FABIUS

You'd know what it is like, soon enough, if Hannibal's army ever marched into Rome.

AMYTIS

I suppose there are no chances of that . . .

FABIUS

No chances whatever, I'm happy to say.

AMYTIS

Are there any women in Rome who have had the misfortune to encounter Hannibal's army?

FABIUS

Oh, yes—we have a great many refugees in the city—pitiful creatures they are, too.

AMYTIS

I'd like to ask some of them up to dinner some time. Their comments might be interesting.

FABIUS

Hannibal will be made to pay for his atrocities.

(*From the far distance, a bugle call is heard— a shrill, weird, barbaric sound, repeated twice in quick succession.* AMYTIS *starts as she hears it, and looks up curiously.*)

AMYTIS

What was that?

FABIUS (*yawning*)

Oh, probably some shepherd (FABIA *enters*) bringing his flocks in from the fields. (*He sits down wearily at the left.*)

FABIA

Fabius, my son, you are tired. You must go to bed and rest. Remember that every ounce of your vigor must be conserved.

AMYTIS

Yes, Fabius—you *must* conserve your vigor.

FABIA

For now you belong to Rome.

FABIUS

Very well, mother dear. I have no choice but to obey. (*He rises and goes to* AMYTIS.)

AMYTIS

Good-night, Fabius, and don't be too annoyed at my ignorance. I'll try to learn. And when Hannibal's head is mounted in the market-place, I shall be there to jeer at his sad face.

FABIUS

Of *course* you will, Amytis. For all your talk, you're just as patriotic as any one. Isn't she, mother?

FABIA (*without enthusiasm*)

I'm sure she is.

FABIUS

Good-night, Amytis, my love. (*He kisses* AMY-TIS *and crosses to* FABIA.) Good-night, mother dear. (*He starts to go out at the left. At the door, he pauses and turns.*) Some day, perhaps, we'll all go to a play. (*He goes out.*)

FABIA

But it will not be "Œdipus Rex." (*She addresses* AMYTIS.) Are you going to bed? (AMY-TIS *doesn't answer.*) Are you going to bed?

AMYTIS

I think I'll stay out here for a while. The air is very pleasant.

FABIA

I advise you to put something around your shoulders. Good-night.

AMYTIS

Good-night, mother—and sweet dreams to *you*. (FABIA *goes out.* META *and* VARIUS *come in timidly from the right.*)

META

My lady . . . Varius and I would like to go for a little walk. May we?

AMYTIS

Of course you may. I wish I could go with you —but I'm afraid it wouldn't look quite right.

VARIUS (*smiling*)

I'm afraid not, my lady.

AMYTIS

You two would like to be married, wouldn't you?

VARIUS

Yes, my lady, we would. Our fathers destined us for each other when we were small children.

META (*hastily*)

But it's out of the question, now, of course.

AMYTIS

I know. Slaves aren't allowed to marry in Rome. That's one of our best laws.

(VARIUS *steps forward, with sudden determination.*)

VARIUS

Might I speak to you, my lady . . .

META (*sensing his purpose*)

No, Varius—you mustn't . . .

AMYTIS

Why, of course you may, Varius.

VARIUS

We want to get away . . .

META (*terrified*)

Varius. Don't! Please don't say it . . .

VARIUS (*desperately*)

We want to escape, my lady. We want to be free.

AMYTIS (*caressingly*)

You want to be free!

META

We know it can't be done, my lady. (*Angrily*) Varius—you're a fool to say these things.

AMYTIS

Not at all, Meta. You and Varius can say anything you please—to me. You needn't be afraid that I'll tell . . . (*she glances toward the left*) . . . anyone.

VARIUS

Then you'll help us to escape?

AMYTIS

I'm afraid that's quite another matter. If I could help you, I would do so. You know I would. But where can you go? Where can you find freedom?

META

I told him that, my lady. I told him it was hopeless. But he would blurt this out.

VARIUS

There are the Carthaginians, my lady. They're friendly to all enemies of Rome.

AMYTIS

The Carthaginians themselves will soon be slaves, Varius. They're to be conquered, like all the others who have tried to argue with Roman supremacy. . . . Rome can't be beaten—not yet. There's an air of destiny about this place, an intimation of empire—and it can't be subdued.

VARIUS

Then there is no hope for us?

AMYTIS

No. We have the misfortune to be thoughtful people—and there's no place for us in the world, as Rome is organizing it. We haven't that air of destiny, nor the self-confident strength that it gives. Thoughtful people are never very successful.

(*The distant bugle call is heard again.* AMYTIS, VARIUS, *and* META *pause to listen to it; there is a sense of vague, suppressed excitement.*)

AMYTIS

There's that strange sound again. What *is* it? (*A loud knocking is heard at the left.*)

AMYTIS

See who that is, Varius.

VARIUS

Yes, my lady.

AMYTIS

Whoever it is, I've gone to bed. (*She goes hurriedly into the sleeping quarters at the left.* VARIUS *goes out at the left, upstage. He is heard to unbolt and open the door, and then to say,* "What is it, Cato?" CATO *replies, excitedly,* "You can see them plainly from the walls—thousands of our men." *They are both speaking together, and their words are therefore indistinct.* VARIUS *returns with* CATO, *an excited youth.*)

CATO (*to* META)

There are hundreds of camp-fires off to the east.

(VARIUS *climbs up one of the columns so that he can see over the top of the low roof.*)

META

What can it be?

VARIUS

The army must have returned.

META

But I thought the army was away, fighting Hannibal.

CATO

They were.   This must mean that they've conquered him, at last.

META

Poor Hannibal!   (*Another loud summons is heard at the left.*)

VARIUS (*climbing down*)

Open the gate, Cato.

(CATO *goes out at the left, and again a confusion of voices is heard—*CATO *saying, "What's happened, sir? You're wounded," and* SCIPIO *saying, "Is Fabius here? I must see Fabius, at once!"* SCIPIO *comes in, with* CATO *following.* SCIPIO *is a handsome young man, wearing the helmet, breastplate, etc., of a Roman officer. His cloak is torn, dirty, and spotted with blood. His left arm is bandaged. He is a fine, upstanding type of soldier—earnest, sincere, intense—one of the men who aided materially in Rome's conquest of the world.*)

Scipio (*steadying himself against a column*)
Summon your master at once.

(Varius *exits into the sleeping quarters.*
Scipio *crosses to the table and slumps down wearily into a chair.* Meta *hands him a goblet of wine.*)

META

We have seen the campfires, sir. Has the army returned?

SCIPIO

Some of it has returned.

(Fabius *comes in, drawing his toga about him.*
He is followed by Varius.)

FABIUS

Scipio, why are you here? What does this mean?

SCIPIO

It means that the Roman army has suffered a terrible defeat.

FABIUS (*bewildered*)

Defeat? Where?

SCIPIO

At Cannæ. We were routed—disgraced!

(Varius *again climbs up the column to look out.*)

FABIUS (*aghast*)

And Hannibal—where is he?

SCIPIO

Hannibal is at the gates of Rome!

VARIUS (*excitedly*)

Then those are Hannibal's camp-fires!

FABIUS

But—but it can't be! It's impossible! Hannibal is two hundred miles from Rome.

SCIPIO

I tell you, Hannibal is at the gates!

META

Do you hear that, Varius? Hannibal is at the gates!

(FABIUS *sits down helplessly.*)

FABIUS (*almost sobbing*)

Hannibal—at the gates—at the gates of Rome. What is it, Scipio? What has happened?

SCIPIO

The Roman army has been wiped out. Our strength and our prestige are gone. Hannibal rules the world.

FABIUS

What shall we do? What shall we do?

SCIPIO (*rising*)

You are the dictator, Fabius. It is for you to decide.

FABIUS (*dully*)

Yes, I am the dictator. It is for me to decide. (*He stands up, making a tremendous effort to pull himself together.*)

FABIUS

Go, Cato, and summon Sertorius, Tibullus, and Drusus, if you can find them.

CATO

Yes, sir!

FABIUS

Tell them to come here at once.

CATO

Yes, sir! (*He runs out. FABIA appears, greatly annoyed at this unusual disturbance.*)

FABIA

What *is* all this racket? Varius, what are you doing up on the roof?

VARIUS

I'm looking at Hannibal.

FABIA

Is Hannibal up there, on the *roof?*

FABIUS

Hannibal is at the gates of Rome.

(*AMYTIS comes in hurriedly, from the left.*)

AMYTIS

What's all this about Hannibal?

FABIUS (*desperately*)

Do I have to say it again?

SCIPIO

Our army has been defeated. Hannibal has marched to Rome. He will occupy the city at any moment.

AMYTIS (*apparently delighted*)

You don't *mean* it!

VARIUS

It's true, my lady. The sky is dark with the smoke of his camp-fires.

AMYTIS

So Hannibal got here, after all.

FABIUS

Yes—and it means death to us all—the end of everything for Rome.

AMYTIS

Think of it. . . . Hannibal!

FABIUS

Rome has been betrayed by the gods.

AMYTIS

Why don't you sit down, Scipio? You must be fearfully tired.

SCIPIO (*ungraciously*)

I'm perfectly able to stand, thank you. (*It is obvious that he bears no love for* AMYTIS, *an attitude that is not uncommon among the friends of* FABIUS.)

FABIUS

Is there any remnant of the army left, Scipio?

SCIPIO

None, Fabius. We were annihilated at Cannæ. A few of us cut our way back to Rome, but even then we travelled no faster than Hannibal with his entire army. He is a superman—a god— against whom mortal strength is of no avail.

AMYTIS

A god!

FABIUS

But I can't understand it, Scipio. Superman

or no superman—we outnumbered his army two
to one. I thought we had him caught in a trap.

SCIPIO

Hannibal let us think so. He forced us to attack the center of his line, where his weakest
troops were massed. He allowed us to drive
through—and then surrounded us, with his infantry and Numidian cavalry.

FABIUS

More of his damnable deception.

AMYTIS

We would never have resorted to such foul tactics—would we, Fabius?

FABIUS

Never!

AMYTIS (*sits*)

No—we wouldn't have thought of them.

(FABIUS *paces up and down in a turmoil of
baffled rage, nervous apprehension and utter be-
wilderment.*)

SCIPIO

I saw Hasdrubal, the Numidian cavalry leader,
cut down dozens of our men with his own sword.
He fought like a fiend, sent down by the gods to
punish us.

AMYTIS

And did you see Hannibal?

SCIPIO

I saw him in the distance.

AMYTIS

What was he doing?

SCIPIO

He was standing on a little hill . . .

FABIUS

Laughing, I suppose?

SCIPIO

No—he was not laughing. He was watching the battle as though it were a play that he had written, being performed by actors in a theatre.

AMYTIS

Is Hannibal good-looking?

SCIPIO

Hannibal's personal appearance did not interest me at the moment.

FABIUS

This is a serious matter, Amytis. I must ask you not to bother us with irrelevant questions now . . .

AMYTIS

But this isn't irrelevant. It is very important for Hannibal to be handsome. Think of the statues.

FABIUS

What else happened, Scipio?

SCIPIO

They closed in on us and butchered us . . . and all through the battle their terrible African war drums kept on beating—louder—louder . . .

AMYTIS (*without enthusiasm*)

It must have been thrilling!

SCIPIO

Our army was a confused mass of struggling, writhing men—battling against an enemy that attacked from every side. The slaughter was unspeakably awful. . . . When it was over, at last, seventy thousand Romans lay dead on the field of Cannæ.

AMYTIS (*slowly*)

Seventy thousand! Why did they die?

SCIPIO (*bitterly*)

Ask Hannibal why they died.

FABIUS

Seventy thousand! What horror! What is this terrible thing the gods have done to us, Scipio—to us who have made our sacrifices regularly in the temple and have spared no effort to show our gratitude for past favors. I can't understand it.

AMYTIS

Perhaps Hannibal was nice to the gods, too.

FABIUS (*vehemently*)

Hannibal's gods are false gods!

AMYTIS

Oh—I see.

SCIPIO

You must take immediate action, Fabius. Hannibal may advance on the city at any moment.

AMYTIS

Can't you possibly keep him out?

FABIUS

No. Rome is doomed. We have no more than five thousand men to defend the walls—and what are five thousand men against Hannibal?

SCIPIO

Every Roman is prepared to fight to the last.

FABIUS

But our women—what of them? You must escape, both of you, while there is still time. My mother and my wife must be spared.

AMYTIS

Spared from what?

FABIUS

From the bestiality of Hannibal's men.

AMYTIS

And are all the Carthaginians so—so extremely warm-blooded?

FABIUS

They're all utterly ruthless. When they enter the city, not one of our women will escape.

AMYTIS

It ought to be quite an experience for the women of Rome.

FABIUS

You must leave the city at once, Amytis.

AMYTIS

And how about you, Fabius?

FABIUS

I am prepared to die—but I am a man.

FABIA

And I, too, am prepared to die. I am a Roman! Here I was born, here I have lived and borne children, here I shall die.

AMYTIS (*rises*)

Well, I am *not* prepared to die! I am not a Roman. I was not born here—and I have certainly borne no children, here or anywhere else. I shall go to Ostia and join my mother.

SCIPIO (*scornfully*)

Spoken like a true Greek.

AMYTIS

Oh, I know it, Scipio—I'm a contemptible coward, but I can't help it. I love life, even monotonous life, and I can't bear to part with it. ⟨
. . . Do you feel bitterness against me, Fabius, because I am not as brave as your mother?

FABIUS

No, Amytis—but it would be beautiful if we were to die together.

AMYTIS

I'm sorry, Fabius, but that's not my idea of beauty. I must confess that I shudder at the thought.

FABIA (*coming forward*)

At last I have an excuse to tell you what I

think of you. I've tried to see the best in you, because you were my son's wife. But there is no best in you. You, who were honored with the love of a good man, have thrown it aside, flippantly. You have put on the airs of a goddess, and displayed the morals . . .

FABIUS

Mother!

FABIA

I hate you—I hate you—and I'm glad that the clean streets of Rome are not to be soiled with your vile blood.

FABIUS

Mother! You musn't say such things to Amytis. She's sensitive.

AMYTIS

No, Fabius, I'm not sensitive. I don't mind. In fact, I'm glad that your mother has finally had the chance to deliver herself on this subject. It's been worrying her for a long time. I've noticed that.

FABIA

Oh, you've pulled the wool over my poor son's eyes. You've fooled him, all right, with your artificial beauty and your false Athenian superiority. Now, thank the gods, he sees you as you are—a heartless, soulless traitor!

(FABIUS *forces her into a chair at the left.*)

AMYTIS

I may be a traitor to Rome, but I am not a
traitor to my own convictions. I didn't start this
war. I've never given it my support or encour-
agement. I have no axe to grind with Hannibal.
Why should I sacrifice my life merely because the
Roman army has failed to subdue a weaker
enemy?

FABIUS (*wearily*)

If you feel that way about it, you'd better go.

AMYTIS

I'm afraid I must, Fabius. You wouldn't want
me to stay and be—whatever you call it, would
you?

FABIUS

Don't speak of it, Amytis. It's unthinkable.

AMYTIS

Yes—one must draw the line somewhere. . . .
Varius, go bring out the horses—the fastest
horses in the stable.

VARIUS

Yes, my lady. (*He dashes out.*)

AMYTIS

Meta, come and help me make ready for the
journey. We mustn't waste a moment.

FABIA

Luckily, Rome does not have to suffer because
of your cowardice.

AMYTIS

Yes, mother—and Rome would gain nothing by my bravery if I were to stay and offer up my beautiful white body. . . . Come on, Meta. (*She and* META *go out at the left.*)

FABIUS

Go see if you can help her, mother.

FABIA

I'll do nothing of the kind. I shall go to the kitchen, and with my own hands I shall prepare some broth for you, my son—my true, Roman son. (*She embraces him and goes out at the right.*)

FABIUS (*in desperation*)

I can't face this calamity, Scipio. Somehow, it doesn't seem right. The gods know we've done nothing to deserve this.

SCIPIO

Hannibal is greater than the gods. We may despise him as an enemy—we may do all in our power to discredit him—but no Roman sword will ever cut the laurel wreath of genius from his brow. (*The rattle of the bolt on the street door is heard.*)

FABIUS

I could well afford to see Hannibal, laurel wreath and all, at the bottom of the Tiber.

(*Enter* SERTORIUS, *an elderly senator, and* DRUSUS, *an equally elderly general. They greet* FABIUS *formally.*)

Have you heard the terrible news from Cannæ?

Drusus

All Rome has heard it by now. Every house in the city is draped with mourning for the dead, and great crowds are gathered in the market-place, weeping hysterically and sending up cries for mercy to the gods.

Fabius

It will do them no good. The gods are in Hannibal's camp to-day.

Sertorius

There is no telling what horrors the people may commit in their madness. What are we to do?

Fabius

What *is* there to do? Hannibal holds us in the hollow of his hand.

(Tibullus *comes in, followed by* Cato. Tibullus *is obviously agitated.*)

Tibullus

You must take decisive action, Fabius. You must *do* something!

Fabius

If we could only delay for a few days, we might recall our army from the siege of Capua.

Tibullus

Delay is out of the question. Hannibal will attack before morning!

Drusus

We couldn't possibly get our army back from Capua in less than two weeks.

SERTORIUS

By that time, Rome will be a mass of smoking ruins.

FABIUS

I suppose it's hopeless.

(AMYTIS *enters, followed by* META, *who carries a large bundle.*)

AMYTIS

Good evening, gentlemen. I hope that you are all enjoying this fine day.

SERTORIUS

Unfortunately, the smoke of Hannibal's camp-fires interferes with the view.

AMYTIS

Well, I must be off for the sea coast, to spend a quiet holiday with my mother. I hope to find you all here when I get back.

FABIUS

Amytis! How can you be so callous?

AMYTIS

Can you blame me for being cheerful in the face of danger? You might try it yourself. If Hannibal should march into Rome, and find you all laughing, he might forget what he came for and join in the merriment.

SCIPIO

Hannibal does not laugh.

(VARIUS *enters from the left.*)

VARIUS

The horses are ready, my lady.

AMYTIS

Then we must start.

FABIUS (*tremulously*)

Good-bye, Amytis. I'm afraid I shall never see
you again.

AMYTIS

Don't say that, Fabius. Hannibal hasn't conquered Rome yet. There is still hope.

FABIUS

Hope is a poor defense against the Numidian
cavalry.

AMYTIS

It's the only defense you have, isn't it?

FABIUS

Yes, I suppose so. We're doomed.

AMYTIS

Had you ever thought of treating with Hannibal?

DRUSUS

What do you mean?

AMYTIS

I mean—why don't you go out, under a flag
of truce, meet Hannibal and talk the thing over
in a civilized manner. He sounds to me like the
type of man who might listen to reason.

Fabius

I wonder if he would?

Scipio (*indignantly*)

Nonsense! Hannibal talks only on the field of battle, with words of steel. The Roman does not live who can argue with him successfully there.

Drusus

Scipio is right. We'll have to fight it out.

Sertorius

We can at least show him that Romans know how to die. (*From a distance, the faint sound of many drums is heard, beating rhythmically, ominously.*)

Fabius (*starting*)

What's that?

Scipio

It's the drums—the African war drums.

Tibullus (*hysterically*)

O, gods of Rome—save us! Save us!

Fabius

The gods can't hear you, Tibullus.

Amytis

In that case, I had better hurry. I don't even know how to die gracefully. . . . (*Fabia enters from the right.*) Good-bye, my husband. Don't eat too much starchy food while I'm away. Good-bye, mother. Good-bye, gentlemen. Good-bye, good-bye. . . . (*She goes out with the two slaves*

at the left. FABIA is still standing at the right,
gazing after the departed AMYTIS.)

FABIUS

Now let's get down to business. (*He sits down,*
surrounded by the others. The sound of the
drums becomes slightly louder, more emphatic.)
We must concentrate our infantry outside the
city walls, prepared to withstand the first shock
of assault . . .

FABIA

Fabius . . .

FABIUS (*paying no attention*)

Our cavalry, such as it is, can be held within
the city, prepared to make a sortie through the
east gate when the situation becomes desperate . . .

FABIA

Fabius . . .

FABIUS (*still not listening*)

You, Drusus, will take command of the infantry on the left . . .

FABIA (*louder*)

Fabius!

FABIUS

And you, Scipio. . . . What is it, mother?

FABIA

Did you notice anything about Amytis when
she left?

FABIUS

She seemed to be in a hurry.

FABIA

Did you notice anything strange in her appearance?

FABIUS (*impatiently*)

No, I did not.

FABIA

She was wearing that new green silk dress!

FABIUS (*not interested*)

She was, was she? . . . Now, if Hannibal attacks us on the right, you, Scipio, will move forward to meet him in pitched battle. If he concentrates on the left. . . . The—the green dress, eh! Isn't that a rather strange costume for travelling. . . . (*In the distance, the war drums continue to beat their weird tattoo as the*

CURTAIN FALLS.)

ACT II

ACT II

Three bugle calls are heard—the curtain rising during the third call.

The scene is HANNIBAL'S *headquarters in a temple, about a mile east of Rome. The temple, normally open, has been converted into a sort of tent by means of rich, crimson draperies, which form the background of the scene. These draperies have been parted so as to form a wide entrance, upstage and slightly to the right, through which the Italian landscape is dimly visible. Characters coming through this entrance walk up two steps to reach the stage.*

There is another entrance at the extreme right, downstage. At the left, downstage, a corner of the inner temple juts out. This is used as HANNIBAL'S *sleeping quarters, and is entered through a door. There is a fourth entrance, upstage left, between the corner of the inner temple and the draperies at the back.*

To the left, and slightly upstage, is a huge column; there are two other columns, of equal size, at either side of the main entrance, although these are largely masked by the draperies.

At the right are a triangular table and two chairs, painted in weird colors and designs. By the column, at the left, are a chair and a massive chest. There is another chest at the back, to the left of the main entrance.

It is night—an hour later than the conclusion of Act I—and two braziers are burning dimly, one at the left and another at the right.

Although the scene is a Roman temple, and although it is probable that HANNIBAL *did not carry many household effects with him on his long march, strict realism and logic may be sacrificed for purposes of dramatic effectiveness in this scene. The barbaric splendor of Carthage itself must be reflected in all the trappings in this distant camp; the audience must feel that the action of the play has shifted from the virtuous but unimaginative simplicity of Rome to the Oriental opulence of its enemies.*

The headquarters guard, consisting of a COR-PORAL *and five stalwart Carthaginian privates, is lined up for inspection by the* SERGEANT, *who is examining their breastplates and swords to see that the metal is well polished, and their hands and faces to make sure that they are clean.*

The SERGEANT *is a rough, husky, brutal veteran, whose counterpart is to be found on every drill ground from Quantico to Aldershot.*

The GUARDSMEN *are fine, upstanding soldiers
—young, vigorous, confident, and cheerful. By
their immediate appearance, they must suggest an
emphatic contrast to the hopeless depression of*
FABIUS *and the other old men in Rome. There is
an eloquently triumphant air about them. In
their speech they are tough and hard-boiled, exactly in the manner of the corporals in "What
Price Glory," it being not unreasonable to assume
that professional soldiers twenty-one hundred
years ago did not differ materially from the professional soldiers of to-day. Their uniforms are
neat, but they show signs of long and arduous
wear.*

The SERGEANT *passes down the line, starting
with the* CORPORAL *at the left, and ending with
the* FIRST GUARDSMAN *at the right. He inspects
the swords and equipment of the men. One helmet
is on crooked; the* SERGEANT *unceremoniously
straightens it.*

At the table sits THOTHMES, *the Egyptian
clerk, a wizened little old man who laboriously
inscribes characters with a brush on sheets of
papyrus, paying no attention to the others.*

SERGEANT (*to the* FIRST GUARDSMAN)
Look at the rust on that sword. Haven't you
been in the army long enough to know how to
keep your arms clean?

FIRST GUARDSMAN (*very weakly*)

Yes, Sergeant. I cleaned it thoroughly this morning. It got rusty during dinner.

SERGEANT

During dinner! Were you *eating* with it?

FIRST GUARDSMAN

No, Sergeant. I was cutting oranges. You can't imagine how those oranges stain the steel.

SERGEANT

Never mind about the oranges. See that it's clean before the chief gets here. If he catches you with a sword like that, you'll do a turn with the elephants.

FIRST GUARDSMAN

Yes, Sergeant.

(*The* SERGEANT *notices something about the* SECOND GUARDSMAN's *face. He steps up to him for closer scrutiny.*)

SERGEANT

Did you wash your face?

SECOND GUARDSMAN

Yes, Sergeant.

SERGEANT

When? While we was crossing the Alps, I suppose. . . . It's about time you went over it again.

SECOND GUARDSMAN

Yes, Sergeant.

SERGEANT

Now listen to this, you men. The commander-in-chief is inspecting the army, and he'll be through any minute now. There's going to be a meeting here of the general staff, Hannibal, Hasdrubal, and all the rest. You've got to be on the job, do you get that? You'll act as runners when you're needed. You'll be in charge, Corporal, 'till I get back.

CORPORAL

Yes, Sergeant.

SERGEANT

Keep two of the men on post outside headquarters, and see that the rest behave themselves. (*He addresses the* FIRST GUARDSMAN.) And *you* —don't you litter up this place with no orange peels, neither.

FIRST GUARDSMAN

No, Sergeant.

(*The* SERGEANT *stalks out, this being the signal for general relaxing by the guardsmen.*)

THIRD GUARDSMAN (*sweetly*)

Good-bye, Sergeant. Come back soon.

(*The* CORPORAL *steps out of line and faces the squad.*)

CORPORAL (*to* FOURTH *and* FIFTH GUARDSMEN)

You men follow me. The rest of you, fall out. (*He goes out at the left with the two guardsmen. The other three break ranks and sit down.*)

FIRST GUARDSMAN (*drawing his sword and exhibiting it*)

Look! He calls that rusty.

THIRD GUARDSMAN

Well, I wouldn't exactly call it spotlessly clean myself.

FIRST GUARDSMAN (*polishing his sword*)

It's a fine army, all right. They expect you to mop up the whole of Italy and keep clean at the same time.

THIRD GUARDSMAN

That's all right. You heard what the Sergeant said about the chief. If *he* catches you with a rusty sword, you'll be doing a turn with the elephants.

FIRST GUARDSMAN

I don't do no turn with no elephants, see? Not while old Hannibal is running this army. I'm Hannibal's little favorite, I am. He's very, very fond of me. Hannibal wants me right here on headquarters staff where I can look out for him.

SECOND GUARDSMAN

I'm certainly glad to hear that. I always wondered who was really the brains of this army.

THIRD GUARDSMAN

Just the same, I'd arrange to keep that knife clean, if I was you. Them elephants need a lot of attention—and Hannibal don't like to have 'em neglected.

SECOND GUARDSMAN

Sure. He put his own brother in command of the elephant brigade, didn't he?   His own brother.

FIRST GUARDSMAN

Oh, I know why Mago got that assignment. Hannibal didn't want anyone to think he's playing favorites. He gives his own brother the rottenest job in the army just to show how impartial he is.

THIRD GUARDSMAN

I've felt sorry for the poor kid. He's been wet nursing those damned elephants now for two years.

FIRST GUARDSMAN

At first, he seemed to be fond of 'em.

SECOND GUARDSMAN

Yeh—I was with the elephant brigade when we was quartered on the Rhone: Well, it seems that there was some sort of funny business among the elephants, and one of the females got—you know —in a family way . . .

THIRD GUARDSMAN

She *did?*

SECOND GUARDSMAN

Well, we got orders to move across the river, and young Mago comes up to the chief and says,

"Hannibal," he says, "we can't move yet. One of my elephants is about to become a mother." And Hannibal says, "That's interesting, but what are we going to do about it? Do you think we ought to hold up the army 'till the child is born?" And young Mago says, "Yes, brother, I think we should, because that elephant ought not to be moved, not in her condition." Well, sir, Hannibal tried not to laugh, and he finally told the kid, "Mago," he says, "we've got a very important war on our hands, and however much we may sympathize with this poor, wayward elephant, I'm afraid we can't afford to wait for her. . . ." You know how long it takes an elephant to come across, don't you?

FIRST GUARDSMAN

No.

SECOND GUARDSMAN

Seven years!

THIRD GUARDSMAN

We'd have been there yet. . . . I guess young Mago has felt sorry sometimes that he *is* Hannibal's brother. The chief keeps his eye on him too much. Mago would like to have some fun with the women like the rest of us, but Hannibal won't let him.

FIRST GUARDSMAN

Hannibal thinks his own brother ought to be above such things.

THIRD GUARDSMAN

Ah—the chief don't know what it is to have a good time.

FIRST GUARDSMAN

Well, it's all right with me, as long as us privates can have it—when we can get it.

SECOND GUARDSMAN

If you ask me, Mago and the rest of the officers ain't been missing much. The women around here in Italy are terrible. They ain't got no originality at all!

THIRD GUARDSMAN

Just wait 'till I get back to Carthage!

FIRST GUARDSMAN

Yes—just wait. We've been on the road for four years now, and it don't look as if this war would ever be over.

THIRD GUARDSMAN (*sauntering over to the right*)

Don't you worry about that. This war is over now. (*He points out at the right.*) Do you see what's over there on them hills? Do you know what that is? That's Rome! That's the place we've come all this way to get—and we're going to get it! When we've cleaned up that job, we're all going home.

SECOND GUARDSMAN

Don't talk to me about Rome. It's the biggest disappointment of my life. Why, I expected to see a real city, with big palaces, all made out of

marble and gold and jewelry. I thought I'd
take home enough souvenirs to keep me and the
missus in luxury for the rest of our lives . . .
and just look at the little dump! We'll be lucky
to pick up a square meal in the whole town.

FIRST GUARDSMAN

It's your own fault, soldier. You *would* see the
world.

(*The* THIRD GUARDSMAN *has wandered over to
the table where* THOTHMES *is writing. He looks
over the Egyptian's shoulder.*)

THIRD GUARDSMAN

What are you writing at now, Gyppy?

THOTHMES (*in a very deliberate, precise manner*)

I am compiling the official record of the battle
of Cannæ.

SECOND GUARDSMAN

You've got a fine job, Gyppy. We fight the
battles, and you write 'em.

THOTHMES

*Some*body has to do this work in the army.

FIRST GUARDSMAN

Yes—and they always manage to find some
damned Egyptian to do it.

THIRD GUARDSMAN

And somebody else has to do the dirty work—
and wouldn't you know they'd pick on me for a
job like that!

THOTHMES

You young men should realize that these records of mine have intense historical value. I have here the entire story of Hannibal's march.

SECOND GUARDSMAN

Don't talk to me about history. I'm getting pretty damned sick of parading around the world making history for somebody else to read.

THIRD GUARDSMAN (*looking about him*)

Say—what kind of a place is this, anyway?

FIRST GUARDSMAN

It's a temple, ain't it, Gyppie?

THOTHMES

It's the temple of the Vestal Virgins. Each year the Roman High Priests select six maidens to guard the sacred flame——

THIRD GUARDSMAN

Vestal Virgins, eh! (*He starts toward the door, left.*) Well—let's have a look around. (*He opens the door and peers in.*)

SECOND GUARDSMAN

He lookin' for virgins. *There's* an optimist! —You'd better keep out of there, soldier. That's Hannibal's sleeping quarters. (*The* THIRD GUARDSMAN *closes the door hurriedly.*)

(*Enter the* CORPORAL.)

CORPORAL

Watch yourselves, boys. Old Hasdrubal is coming up the hill. There's going to be one of

them conferences here. 'Tshun! (*He salutes as*
HASDRUBAL *strides in. HASDRUBAL is the sec-*
ond in command of the Carthaginian army—a
dark, ominous, explosive, fire-eating cavalry offi-
cer, who moves with a jerky rapidity that indi-
cates intense nervous energy. He glares at the
three guardsmen.)

HASDRUBAL

Is Hannibal here yet?

CORPORAL

No, sir. He hasn't come yet. He's down . . .

HASDRUBAL (*barking out his words*)

What are you men doing here? Why aren't
you out making yourselves useful?

CORPORAL

We were posted here by the Sergeant, sir.

HASDRUBAL (*with withering sarcasm*)

Oh—I see. This army is being commanded by
sergeants, eh?

CORPORAL

That seems to be the general impression, sir
—among the sergeants.

HASDRUBAL

You can convey my humble apologies to the
Sergeant. Tell him I thought you might be more
useful digging latrines, or any other damned thing
you can think of. But DON'T STAND AROUND! Do
you grasp that?

CORPORAL

Yes, sir.

HASDRUBAL

Very well, then. Get out!

CORPORAL

Yes, sir. Hup! (*The* CORPORAL *and the three guardsmen march out.* HASDRUBAL *turns to* THOTHMES, *who is still writing laboriously.*)

HASDRUBAL

And you, too. You'll have to find some other place to do your home work.

THOTHMES

But I was told . . .

HASDRUBAL

Never mind what you were told. I'm telling you something else. Get out!

THOTHMES

Very well, sir. (THOTHMES *gathers up his sheets of papyrus and his writing utensils.*)

(HASDRUBAL *sits down at the table and spreads out a map, which he proceeds to study.*)

(CARTHALO *and* MAHARBAL *enter.* CARTHALO *is a rough, bluff old warrior;* MAHARBAL *is a gaunt, hard, cynical strategist.*)

(THOTHMES *goes out, with an apprehensive glance toward* HASDRUBAL.)

CARTHALO

Hello, Hasdrubal. Is the chief here yet?

HASDRUBAL

No, there was no one here but some damned guardsmen. They told me they couldn't leave because they'd been posted by a sergeant. . . . Oh, how I hate staff sergeants!

MAHARBAL

We've got to have sergeants, Hasdrubal. That's just one of the many inconveniences of war.

CARTHALO

The chief has been down inspecting my divisions. He certainly does look tired.

MAHARBAL

He's been through the whole army since we pulled in this afternoon, examining the equipment and the food and talking to the men.

HASDRUBAL

I wish I had his patience. It seems to be a physical impossibility for me to talk to a private without losing my temper.

(*Enter* MAGO *wearily. He is* HANNIBAL'S *younger brother—a personable youth, well set up and handsome. At the start of the campaign, he had been terribly enthusiastic and overwhelmed by the craving for adventure, but most of the thrill has worn off by now. Nevertheless, he is still fresh and jaunty, with an irrepressible self-assurance.*)

CARTHALO and MAHARBAL

Hello, Mago . . .

MAGO

Hello, Hasdrubal—hello. . . . (*He sinks down
wearily on a chair at the left.*)

CARTHALO

Well, Mago—how are the elephants?

MAGO

Don't speak of those damned elephants. I've
just had 'em bathed, and fed, and their tusks polished. I've put 'em to bed, and sung 'em lulla-
bies . . . and I'm tired out.

HASDRUBAL

Did you see Hannibal?

MAGO

Oh, yes. He's just been down inspecting us.
He wants to make sure that the dear elephants
are entirely comfortable.

CARTHALO

Never mind, Mago. You'll have your reward
to-morrow. You and your elephants will be able
to march into Rome.

MAGO

Do we go in to-morrow? Are we that near?

HASDRUBAL

Of course we are. There's Rome right over
there.

MAGO (*jumping up and going to look*)

So that's Rome, is it? It isn't so much, after all.

MAHARBAL

I wouldn't be too sure that we're going into Rome to-morrow.

HASDRUBAL

Why not? Why should we delay?

MAHARBAL

Hannibal may decide not to occupy the city just yet. He received a message from Capua to-day, asking for help. There's a Roman army there besieging our allies.

HASDRUBAL (*enraged*)

Well, who gives a good goddam for our allies? We've come all this way to destroy Rome, haven't we? And now's our chance, isn't it?

MAHARBAL

You know Hannibal. He makes his own decisions for himself. He doesn't ask our advice.

CARTHALO

He doesn't need it.

HASDRUBAL

Hannibal is insane if he turns away from Rome now. The city is ours. They have only two legions to defend it. We could walk in this minute . . . and if we fail to destroy Rome now, you know what'll happen in Carthage, don't you? They'll turn against Hannibal. He'll be discredited—stripped of his power. . . . Oh, he can't make a mistake like this.

(*The* SERGEANT *is heard, off-stage, to shout* " 'Tshun!" *The four officers snap to it and salute stiffly as* HANNIBAL *enters.*)

(HANNIBAL *is tall, thin, dark—quiet and surprisingly unemphatic in his speech—rather diffident in his manner. He is obviously terribly tired, but he has trained himself to such a point that he can readily ignore fatigue. He is the sort of man who is apparently none too powerful physically, but manages to exist on an inexhaustible supply of reserve strength. He provides not only the brains which direct his army, but the vitality which animates it. He is regarded with absolutely unqualified respect by his officers and men alike; his mildest whisper is instantly obeyed.*)

(HANNIBAL *returns the salute, and then removes his helmet and sword, which he hands to* BALA, *a gigantic Nubian slave, who follows him.* BALA *goes out at the left.*)

(HANNIBAL *walks to the table and sits down, relaxing easily in the chair.*)

HANNIBAL
Have you been looking at Rome?

MAGO
Yes, sir. It's not very impressive.

HANNIBAL
You'll have a closer view to-morrow.

HASDRUBAL (*excitedly*)

Are we going in?

HANNIBAL

We attack the city on the morning.

HASDRUBAL

Thank the gods! We're going in at last!
(*The four officers are obviously delighted at the prospect.*)

MAHARBAL

I was afraid you might decide to turn off and raise the siege of Capua.

HANNIBAL

Capua can wait. The men need a little rest and recreation after all they've been through. The destruction of Rome will be in the nature of harmless diversion.

CARTHALO

Are we going to burn Rome to the ground?

HANNIBAL

I suppose so. That's what we came for, isn't it?

HASDRUBAL

Of course, it is! We'll show those damned Roman upstarts that they can't dispute the supremacy of Carthage. When we get through with Rome, there'll be nothing left of it but a memory.

HANNIBAL (*thinking of something else*)

Nothing left but a memory.

MAGO

I suppose the elephant brigade, as usual, will miss all the fun.

HANNIBAL

On the contrary, Mago, the elephants will lead the procession into the city. I want you to put on your finest uniform, comb your hair, and shave carefully, because we expect you to look your best. We must convince these Roman upstarts, as Hasdrubal calls them, of our importance.

MAGO

I'll have those elephants painted every color in the rainbow.

HANNIBAL

I wouldn't exactly overdo it. We want the Roman citizens to think that we're an army. We mustn't look too much like a circus parade.

HASDRUBAL

They know we're an army, all right. They found that out at Lake Trasimenus and Cannæ.

HANNIBAL

Don't boast about your victories, Hasdrubal. You can save them for your wife when you get home.

HASDRUBAL

Damn it all, sir, you don't seem to get any satisfaction out of anything. You ought to feel proud that our army has beaten the Romans whenever we've met them. You ought to be like

the rest of us and celebrate a victory, now and
then. Sometimes, by the gods, I actually think
you don't care whether we win or lose.

(HANNIBAL *stands up, and walks slowly across
the stage during the following speech.*)

HANNIBAL

It's not quite as bad as all that, Hasdrubal.
I *do* care whether we win or lose. I suppose it's
the only thing I have to care about in the whole
world. . . . But—if we win a victory, that's that.
We have to go on to the next battle, then the next,
and the next, until we've finished this war. Then
we go home to Carthage and start looking for
another.

MAHARBAL

You ought to take a rest, sir.

HANNIBAL

That's just the trouble with victory, Maharbal. You can't rest. You're only allowed to
quit when you're losing. . . . Look at those seventy thousand Roman soldiers we butchered at
Cannæ. They don't care now whether Rome is destroyed or not. Their work is done. They're at
liberty to take a rest—a long rest.

HASDRUBAL

They can have their rest. I'd rather go on
fighting.

HANNIBAL

Of course, Hasdrubal. You're a soldier, and

a damned good one. You live on cavalry charges,
flank movements and counter-attacks; it's your
whole existence.

HASDRUBAL

How about yourself, sir? I haven't noticed
you signing any peace treaties.

HANNIBAL

I know it. But then, I have my oath to think
of—undying hatred of Rome. I have had that
with me ever since I was nine years old, and I
can't very well get rid of it until there's no more
Rome left for me to hate.

CARTHALO

That's the proper spirit, sir. It's much easier
to kill a man if you hate him.

HANNIBAL

Very true, Carthalo, very true. I never thought
of you before as a philosopher.

MAHARBAL

Have you any orders for to-morrow, sir?

HANNIBAL

Never mind them now, Maharbal. They're very
simple, and we can talk them over in the morning.
We all need some rest to-night.

MAHARBAL

You need it most of all, sir. How long is it
since you've had any sleep?

HANNIBAL

Oh, I don't remember. What difference does it make?

MAHARBAL

It would make a great deal of difference to this army if you wrecked your health.

CARTHALO

We couldn't go on, sir.

HASDRUBAL

Don't be a damned fool, sir. For the love of Ba-al, take care of yourself.

HANNIBAL

I thank you, gentlemen, for the vote of confidence, but I can assure you that there's no cause for alarm. I fully expect to survive the destruction of Rome.

MAGO

After that's over, we can all go home, can't we?

HANNIBAL

I hope so.

MAGO (*reflectively*)

I wonder what it will feel like to be back in civilian clothes.

HANNIBAL

You gentlemen can get back to your units, now. See that the men don't sit up all night drinking. They must get some sleep.

HASDRUBAL, MAHARBAL, *and* CARTHALO

Yes, sir. (*They salute and go out.* MAGO *stays behind.*)

MAGO

Can I stay for a while, Hannibal? I get so damned lonely down there with nobody to talk to except the elephants.

HANNIBAL

Yes, Mago, I want you to stay.

MAGO

Have you heard anything from home, lately?

HANNIBAL

Yes—I got a letter from mother to-day. It was sent through Capua and forwarded on here.

MAGO

What does she say?

HANNIBAL

Oh, not much. Everything's just about the same in Carthage. They're all delighted at our victories . . .

MAGO (*bitterly*)

Yes—they're so delighted that they won't do anything to help us. They expect us to get along without reinforcements or supplies or money. I wish some of those damned politicians could see what it's like over here. It might change their attitude about war a little.

HANNIBAL

I think we can manage without their assistance.
(*He rings the gong.*)

MAGO

What else does mother have to say?
(BALA *enters.*)

HANNIBAL

She says that Uncle Hamilcar fell down and
broke his hip again. . . . Here, do you want to
read it? (*He hands* MAGO *the letter.*)

MAGO

Thanks.

HANNIBAL (*to* BALA)

We'll have supper here whenever it's ready.
(BALA *bows and goes out.*)

HANNIBAL (*to* MAGO)

I'm going to try to get clean. Call me when
supper's ready. (HANNIBAL *goes out at the left.*
MAGO *stands, reading the letter. The* SERGEANT
enters briskly and salutes.)

MAGO

What is it, Sergeant?

SERGEANT

We've caught a spy, sir.

MAGO

Well, what of it? Cut his heart out.

SERGEANT

It isn't a he, sir. It's a woman.

MAGO

What sort of a woman?

SERGEANT

A young woman, sir. She says she's a Roman
lady. Not bad-looking, either.

MAGO

Bring her in.

(*The* SERGEANT *goes to the back and calls,*
"Bring 'em in, Corporal." The CORPORAL *enters*
with AMYTIS, VARIUS, *and* META, *accompanied by*
the FIRST *and* SECOND GUARDSMEN, *who have their*
swords drawn. MAGO *continues to read the letter,*
paying little attention to the prisoners.)

MAGO (*to* AMYTIS)

They tell me you're a spy.

AMYTIS

Why, no, sir, I'm not exactly a spy—I . . .

MAGO

Who are those others?

AMYTIS

They're only my slaves—a delightful young
couple from Sicily.

MAGO

Where did you find these people, Sergeant?

SERGEANT

Our sentries picked 'em up, sir. They was
prowling around outside the camp—said they
was refugees from Rome and got lost.

AMYTIS

We were trying to escape from the city, and took the wrong road.

MAGO

That sounds highly improbable. Have you anything more to say for yourself?

AMYTIS

I beg your pardon. Are *you* Hannibal?

MAGO

I am not.

AMYTIS

I didn't really think you were.

MAGO

I happen to be Hannibal's brother, in case you're interested.

AMYTIS

Where is Hannibal? I should love to meet him.

MAGO

I'm afraid that I must deny my brother that pleasure. Sergeant, take these damned Romans out and put 'em to death.

(*The* SERGEANT *steps forward to seize* AMYTIS, *but hesitates when she speaks,*)

AMYTIS

To death! But you can't do that—it—it isn't fair.

VARIUS

You have no right to kill her. She's not an ordinary Roman, she's . . .

AMYTIS

Hush, Varius. (*To* MAGO.) I should like to know who gave you authority to sentence me to death, without a hearing, with no attempt at justice.

MAGO

You know the penalty. You took your chances when you came to spy on us.

AMYTIS

But I didn't . . .

MAGO

You're a Roman, aren't you?

AMYTIS

Of course, I . . .

MAGO

That's all I need to know. You're a **Roman**, an enemy of Carthage. You were caught snooping around within our lines. You'll have to die.

AMYTIS

Can't I even say a word in my own defense?

MAGO

You've said too much already.

AMYTIS

And I can't see Hannibal?

MAGO (*vehemently*)

No! You can't see Hannibal. He has enough to worry about without having to listen to you.

AMYTIS

I suppose I shall have to take your word for it.

(*She turns to* VARIUS *and* META.)   I'm sorry that
you must die.

> META (*clasping* VARIUS' *hand*)

We're not afraid.

AMYTIS

Of course you're not, you poor things.   Roman
slaves haven't much to live for.

VARIUS

But you—my lady—you're not ready to die.

AMYTIS

I'm always ready, Varius. . . . But it *is* a nui-
sance. . . . If I'd only stayed in Rome, I should
have been acclaimed a heroine by my husband and
Scipio and all those stuffy old Senators.   Now,
I must sacrifice my life and get no credit for it.

MAGO

We don't ordinarily bury spies with military
honors, but we might make an exception in your
case.

AMYTIS

I'm sure you'll do the right thing.

MAGO

All right, Sergeant.

SERGEANT

Hup! (*The* SERGEANT, CORPORAL, *and* GUARDS-
MEN *start to lead* AMYTIS, VARIUS, *and* META
out.)

MAGO

Just a minute. Have you searched these people, Sergeant?

SERGEANT (*turning to* CORPORAL)

Have you searched these people, Corporal?

CORPORAL (*turning to the* GUARDSMEN)

Have you searched these people?

FIRST GUARDSMAN

Have you searched these people?

(*The* SECOND GUARDSMAN *turns his head slightly to see whether there is anyone to whom he can pass the buck.*)

SECOND GUARDSMAN

No, sir!

FIRST GUARDSMAN

No, sir!

CORPORAL

No, sir!

SERGEANT

No, sir!

MAGO

Then search 'em quickly. They may have despatches concealed.

(*The* CORPORAL *and the* GUARDSMEN *start to search* VARIUS *and* META. *The* SERGEANT *starts to search* AMYTIS.)

AMYTIS

Do I have to be pawed by this man?

MAGO

Never mind, Sergeant, *I'll* do the searching.

(*The* SERGEANT *leads* AMYTIS *before* MAGO, *who starts to pat her all over, in the manner of a detective frisking a yegg for his gun.* MAGO *stands so that his back is to the left of the stage, which* AMYTIS *faces.* AMYTIS *giggles hysterically.*) What are you laughing at?

AMYTIS

You're tickling me!

(MAGO *completes the search without results, but he still holds* AMYTIS' *shoulders in his hands. He surveys her with interest.*)

MAGO

You know—you're rather beautiful.

AMYTIS

I always try to look my best when going to an execution.

MAGO (*significantly*)

Maybe there won't be any execution, after all. Maybe I'll take you down and show you the elephants. (*At this moment* HANNIBAL *comes in quietly at the left. He sees* MAGO *and* AMYTIS *in the center of the stage,* VARIUS, META, *and the soldiers at the back.* AMYTIS *sees him over* MAGO's *shoulder, but* MAGO *goes right on talking.*) You know, I've been waiting for a long time for someone like you to visit our camp. Hannibal won't let us officers associate with women who are our

social inferiors, but you seem to be real aristoc-
racy, as these things go in Rome. . . . Why do
you keep poking me?

(AMYTIS *points to* HANNIBAL. MAGO *turns
around, sees his brother, and starts guiltily away
from* AMYTIS.)

MAGO (*lamely, as he salutes*)
We caught a spy, sir—a Roman spy.

HANNIBAL
I was wondering . . .

AMYTIS
You're Hannibal, aren't you! (*A statement
rather than a question.*)

HANNIBAL
I am. (HANNIBAL *walks past her and crosses
to the table. Presently* AMYTIS *follows him.*)

AMYTIS (*surveying him*)
So you're Hannibal. . . . You're not the way
I pictured you, at all.

HANNIBAL (*politely*)
I hope I'm not a disappointment.

MAGO
We caught this woman red-handed, sir. She
and these others were trying to sneak through our
lines.

HANNIBAL
That was highly injudicious of you, madam—I
mean, to be caught.

AMYTIS

I realize that now.

MAGO

I cross-examined her.

AMYTIS

He did not. He tickled me.

MAGO

It was my duty, sir, to search her person for any documents that might be of value. She chose to interpret my actions as a personal advance.

AMYTIS

He told me he was going to take me down and show me the elephants (HANNIBAL *laughs*.) Scipio told me you never laugh.

HANNIBAL

Scipio has happened to encounter me only in my less mirthful moments. (*He sits down at the table*.)   I must apologize for my brother, madam. He's very young, and has much to learn about the gentle art of soldiering.

AMYTIS

Oh, that's all right. I understand perfectly. (*To* MAGO.)   You're forgiven.

HANNIBAL

In this delightful conversation that went on between you two, was any mention made of the possible penalty for espionage?

MAGO

Of course there was. I sentenced all three of them to death.

HANNIBAL

Is there any particular reason why this ceremony should be delayed?

MAGO (*looking at* AMYTIS)

There certainly isn't.

HANNIBAL

In that case, Sergeant, you may proceed in the
usual manner.

SERGEANT

Come on you! (*He starts to lead her out.
AMYTIS breaks away from him, goes to the table
at which HANNIBAL is sitting, and speaks directly
to him.*)

AMYTIS

I'm not asking for mercy, Hannibal. I know
that there is no such thing in war.

SERGEANT (*starting for her*)

I told you to come with me.

HANNIBAL

Stand back, Sergeant. Let her talk.

AMYTIS

I'm ready to die—for the glory of Rome, or
whatever it is we're fighting for now. I'm not
afraid—no, I mean that. I'm really not afraid.
That's not heroism, either. It's just the attitude
of stoicism that comes to everyone, I suppose.
You soldiers who have been in battle must know
what I mean.

MAGO

Must we listen to all this?

HANNIBAL

Go on.

AMYTIS

In Athens, when men were condemned to death, they were granted one last request—provided, of course, that it was within reason. If they wanted a sumptuous repast, they could have it. Or they might crave a last hour with their loved ones. They could have that, too. . . . Some of these men were murderers, some traitors, but all were accorded the same final favor. It didn't amount to much—it cost the state nothing. But it did help to send those poor creatures out with a somewhat less anguished conscience. . . . That's what I ask of you, Hannibal—one final favor.

MAGO

Don't listen to her, Hannibal. She's a bad woman.

HANNIBAL

What is it that you want?

AMYTIS (*hesitantly*)

I can't tell you before all these people.

MAGO

I thought not. I tell you, Hannibal, she's dangerous. I wouldn't listen to a word she says.

HANNIBAL

Dismissed, Sergeant. Take these prisoners with you.

SERGEANT

Yes, sir. Hup!

(VARIUS *and* META *are led out by the* CORPO-
RAL *and* GUARDSMEN.)

AMYTIS

Nothing will happen to them . . .?

HANNIBAL

Sergeant, you will be responsible for the safety
of the prisoners.

SERGEANT

Yes, sir . . . (*He salutes and goes out.*)

MAGO

Well—what is it?

AMYTIS (*to* HANNIBAL)

Does *he* have to stay?

HANNIBAL (*smiling*)

You can go, Mago.

MAGO (*ominously*)

I wouldn't do this, Hannibal.

HANNIBAL

Don't worry, Mago. I think I can take care of
myself. She doesn't seem to be armed.

MAGO

She doesn't have to be. (*He goes out. For an
instant,* HANNIBAL *regards* AMYTIS *in silence.
Then he motions her gracefully to a chair across
the table from his.*)

HANNIBAL

Won't you—sit down?

AMYTIS

Thanks.   (*There is an awkward pause after she has seated herself.*)

HANNIBAL

I don't wish to seem peremptory, but I happen to be quite busy these days, and I therefore urge that you come to the point with the least possible delay . . . you'll forgive me, won't you?

AMYTIS

Don't mention it.   I . . .

HANNIBAL

And before you start, I wish to impress upon you the fact that this indignity, to which you are necessarily submitted, is not intended as a personal affront.   Not at all.   We have nothing whatever against you as an individual; at the same time, we can't possibly ignore your status as a representative of Rome.   It's this way: there happens to be a war on just at present, the contending parties being Rome, on the one hand, and Carthage on the other . . .

AMYTIS

Oh, yes.   My husband told me all about that to-day.

HANNIBAL

Your husband should have told you something else before sending you out on this mission, whatever it is.   He should have explained that there is an ancient law of warfare which prescribes instant death for all those caught in the act of espionage.   If we violated that law, we should ourselves be guilty of delinquency, and Carthage would undoubtedly be expelled from the Mediterranean League.

AMYTIS

I appreciate the difficulties of your position.

HANNIBAL

I hoped you would. . . . Now, if you will be so good . . .

AMYTIS

You assume that my husband sent me on this mission.   Do you know who my husband is?

HANNIBAL

I'm afraid I don't.

AMYTIS

He is Quintus Fabius Maximus.

HANNIBAL

Fabius Maximus, eh. . . . One of the consuls.

AMYTIS

One of the consuls nothing.   He's the dictator!

HANNIBAL

Oh, I hadn't heard.   Congratulations.

AMYTIS

My husband didn't send me on this mission.   In fact, he doesn't even know I'm here.   He thinks

I'm on my way to Ostia to join my mother. . . .
You know what's going on in Rome, of course.

HANNIBAL

I hear occasionally from my agents in the city.

AMYTIS

So you use spies, too.

HANNIBAL

Oh, we all do. One of my finest officers is in
Rome this minute, posing as a merchant from
Antioch.

AMYTIS

You don't *say* so. . . . Why, I bought this
dress from him. Do you like it?

HANNIBAL

Charming!

AMYTIS

He has probably informed you that you are not
a particularly welcome guest in these parts.
Why, today, when the cry of "Hannibal is at the
gates" went up, the whole population turned out
to curse you and the gods that brought you here.

HANNIBAL

The gods are blamed for everything.

AMYTIS

I don't want you to think that I'm disloyal to
Rome. I'm not really a Roman at all. I was
born in Athens, and for some reason I've never
been able to understand the Roman ideals of civic
virtue. They think I'm an awful coward. . . .

This evening they asked me to stay and die like a
true Roman. . . .

HANNIBAL

To stay and die?   Is the situation as hopeless
as all that?

AMYTIS

We may as well be frank with each other, Hannibal. You know that the defenses of Rome
haven't a chance against your army, and the Romans know it even better than you do. They've
been desperately afraid of you ever since you
crossed the Alps.

HANNIBAL

I suppose I should feel flattered.

AMYTIS

You should. Today, young Scipio described
you as a superman, a god, against whom mortal
strength is of no avail.   I heard him say it—and
that's why I'm here.

HANNIBAL (*puzzled*)

That's why you're here?

AMYTIS

I wanted, for once in my life, to see a superman.
. . When I left Rome in disgrace, I had no in-
tention of going to visit my mother. That was
just an excuse—I led my slaves along the wrong
road, deliberately. When your sentries captured
me, they wanted to put me to death at once. I
told them I had a message for Hannibal.

(BALA *comes in, bearing a huge tray laden with food for* HANNIBAL *and* MAGO. *He sees* AMYTIS, *looks at her curiously, and then sets the tray down on the table.*)

HANNIBAL

I haven't yet heard what that message is.

AMYTIS

Oh, food! How nice! I'm simply famished! It was very thoughtful of you to have supper for me, Hannibal.

(BALA *serves the meal, and then takes up his position by the column, upstage.*)

HANNIBAL (*elaborately polite*)

I must apologize for the simplicity of the meal. We're living on army rations, you know.

AMYTIS

Army rations! Why, it's de*lic*ious! We never have anything as good as this in Rome. We have to deny ourselves all luxuries on account of the war. . . . What marvellous wine!

HANNIBAL

Yes, the wine is rather good. It's a Spanish wine that we brought with us. There's very little of it left, but we hope to replenish our supply tomorrow.

AMYTIS

In Rome? (HANNIBAL *nods*, AMYTIS *laughs*.) You won't find much of that in Rome . . . or anything else, for that matter.

HANNIBAL

You don't seem to be particularly patriotic.

AMYTIS

That's what my husband has been telling me for five long years.

HANNIBAL

Your husband, I take it, is a true patriot.

AMYTIS

Oh, one hundred per cent—at least.

HANNIBAL

He might be a trifle annoyed if he knew that you were having dinner with the arch-enemy of Rome.

AMYTIS

It takes less than that to annoy him. Poor Fabius! But I can always talk him out of it.

HANNIBAL

He must be very fond of you.

AMYTIS

Oh . . . I suppose so. It's never really been what you'd call an ideal love match. My father left me under Fabius' protection, and our marriage was the inevitable result. Not that I cared, particularly. Being only a half-breed Roman, I had no choice in the matter.

HANNIBAL

Have you never fallen in love with anyone?

AMYTIS

No. . . . I worshipped all the heroes of my-

thology, of course—but that doesn't mean anything.

HANNIBAL

Your husband must be a hero in Rome.

AMYTIS

Possibly. . . . I know I should have been more
appreciative.   He's been a good, kind, consider-
ate husband.   We've got along well together.
He's had his interests and I . . . well, I suppose
it's my own fault that I haven't had mine . . .

HANNIBAL

Any children?

AMYTIS

That's a subject we don't discuss.

HANNIBAL

I beg your pardon.

AMYTIS

Am I boring you with all this?

HANNIBAL

Not at all.   It's a rare treat.   We have so few
opportunities for polite conversation in the army.
. . . But I'm afraid that the Sergeant is growing a trifle impatient out there . . .

AMYTIS

I'd almost forgotten about the Sergeant. And
my slaves, they're out there, too.   Poor things
— they must be dying of hunger.   Couldn't
you . . .?

HANNIBAL

Of course! Bala, see that supper is served for
the two prisoners, at once. They won't have
much more time!

AMYTIS

And some of that Spanish wine, too. They'd
love that.

HANNIBAL

Yes, Bala—get them some of the Spanish wine,
by all means.

(BALA *bows and goes out.*)

AMYTIS

I've completely forgotten what we were talking about.

HANNIBAL

As I remember, we discussed plans for putting
you to death and you asked . . . that's it! You
were going to ask for one final favor.

AMYTIS

Of course!

HANNIBAL

Are you ready now to issue a statement on that
subject?

AMYTIS

Before I do, I should like to ask you just one
question. It may seem like a rather trivial question, but I hope you'll answer it—not as a Carthaginian conqueror speaking to a Roman victim—
but as one civilized human to another.

HANNIBAL

What is the question?

AMYTIS

It is this: Why have you done it?

HANNIBAL

Why have I done it?   Why have I done what?

AMYTIS

Oh, everything that you've done—fighting wars, winning battles . . . why?

HANNIBAL (*after a moment's pause*)

That's a strange question.

AMYTIS

You must know the answer.   You must have had some definite motive to inspire you.

HANNIBAL

But who cares about my motives?   It's only my actual accomplishments that count.

AMYTIS

I care about your motives.

HANNIBAL

Why?

AMYTIS

I just happen to be curious, that's all.

HANNIBAL

I should think that my reasons would be fairly obvious.   I came here to destroy Rome.   Isn't that reason enough?

AMYTIS

Is it enough to satisfy you?

Hannibal

I can't see that that makes any difference.

Amytis

Oh—but it does. It makes an enormous difference. You know, some day you'll have to reason this thing out with yourself. Some day, you'll say to yourself, "Here, I've marched three thousand miles, and crossed mountains and things, and spilt a lot of blood—and what good has it done?" It would be most embarrassing if you suddenly realized that you'd been wasting your time.

Hannibal

I'm not supposed to think about such things. I'm a soldier. I have to content myself with a soldier's rewards.

Amytis

As, for instance?

Hannibal

Well—when I get back to Carthage, I shall receive medals, and testimonial documents, and I shall be the guest of honor at state banquets, and . . .

Amytis

Yes, and they'll give you the key to the city. I know all about that. My husband once was given the key to the city. We have it at home, somewhere. Take my word for it, it doesn't do you any good.

HANNIBAL

I suppose not.   But it's a nice sentiment.

AMYTIS

So that's what you've been striving for—fighting for all these years.   A nice sentiment!

HANNIBAL

If you choose to put it that way—yes.

AMYTIS

No. I don't believe it. You'll have to offer a better reason than that.

HANNIBAL

I'm beginning to sympathize with your husband. . . . By the way, what is your name?

AMYTIS

Amytis.   But why do you sympathize with my husband?

HANNIBAL

I shouldn't care to live with a woman who asked so many questions.

AMYTIS

If you'd only give me an intelligent answer, I'd stop.

(HANNIBAL *rises and crosses to the left.*)

HANNIBAL

Perhaps I can't explain my actions.

AMYTIS

You don't even know yourself?

HANNIBAL

That question of yours disturbed me a little.

. . . I've asked myself that same thing so many times.

AMYTIS

I rather imagined that you had.

HANNIBAL

One morning we were camped on the banks of the Rhone River. It was swollen with the spring floods. I had to get my army across—eighty thousand infantry, cavalry, elephants—with all their supplies. We had no boats of our own; there were no bridges. Across the river, a howling mob of Gauls was waiting to slaughter us as we landed. From the south, a large Roman army was advancing to attack us. . . . I sent a small body of men upstream to get across as best they could and to attack the Gauls on their right flank. I was waiting for the signal from that detachment, and wondering whether I should ever set foot on the opposite bank. . . . As I stood there, I asked myself, "Why do I do this? Even if a miracle occurs, and we do cross the river, what then? What will we have gained?" I didn't know.

AMYTIS

But you did cross the river, didn't you, Hannibal?

HANNIBAL

Yes—we routed the Gauls, and tricked the Romans, and marched on to the Alps. . . . Have you ever tried to lead an elephant over a snow peak?

AMYTIS

No—that's one of the many adventures I've missed.

HANNIBAL

Our men, who were accustomed to the fierce heat of Africa, had to plod through the Alpine snows, many of them in their bare feet. They had to drag the elephants and all the machinery of war with them, while the natives pushed avalanches down on our heads. . . . When we came to the last line of mountains, and saw Italy spread out at our feet, I asked myself that same question. . . . I've never been able to find an answer. I've watched our men slaughter the Romans in one terrible battle after another. Through all these years, I've seen nothing but death—death—and I've never been able to find an answer. (*He crosses over to the right and stands gazing off toward Rome.*)

AMYTIS

Not even in the key to the city?

HANNIBAL

For ten years I've followed the road that leads to Rome—and it's a hard road to travel, Amytis. It's littered with the bones of dead men. Perhaps they know why they died. I don't.

(AMYTIS *rises and stands behind him.*)

AMYTIS

And now you've come to the end of that road, Hannibal. There's your goal—before you. You can see the lights of Rome clearly, can't you? Even the lights seem to tremble with fear of Hannibal. . . . They know that tomorrow they'll be snuffed out forever. . . . Poor little Rome . . .

HANNIBAL

The Romans think that I'm a cruel, merciless enemy. . . . Well, I am.

AMYTIS

You're terribly proud of that, aren't you?

HANNIBAL (*turning to face her*)

Proud of what?

AMYTIS

Of the thought that you're cruel—merciless— a big, terrifying brute.

HANNIBAL

The Romans have inflicted that reputation on me.

AMYTIS

And you're trying hard to live up to it, aren't you?

HANNIBAL

I'm not sorry to have my enemies afraid of me.

AMYTIS

Do you want me to be afraid of you?

HANNIBAL

I should like it better if you were the least bit more respectful.

AMYTIS

Have you any idea why *I* came here?

HANNIBAL

I assume that you're a spy . . . if you are, your methods of gaining information are inexcusably crude.

AMYTIS

I'm not a spy. Can't you believe that? I didn't come here to learn any military secrets. This is nothing but a pleasure trip.

HANNIBAL

A pleasure trip! With swift, violent death staring you in the face?

AMYTIS

I saw the smoke from your camp this afternoon.

HANNIBAL

Well?

AMYTIS

I saw the smoke—and I decided that I should like to see the fire.

HANNIBAL

Evidently you didn't consider the possibility that you might be burned.

AMYTIS

Oh, yes—I thought of that! It made it all the more exciting.

HANNIBAL

You should have waited in Rome. There'll be fire there tomorrow—the fire of divine vengeance.

AMYTIS

Divine vengeance! So you're doing this as a special favor to the gods.

HANNIBAL

The gods are on our side. That's why we're winning.

AMYTIS

You mean, that's why the gods are on your side.

HANNIBAL

I suppose you know that that's sacrilege.

AMYTIS

Call it sacrilege or truth—it's all the same thing. . . . You're afraid of the truth, Hannibal. You're afraid to face it, because the gods tell you to look the other way.

HANNIBAL (*scornfully*)

Are the gods afraid of the truth?

AMYTIS

Of course they are; and they don't want us mortals to be too intimate with it. When we know the truth, we can't know fear—and without fear, there can be no gods. . . .

HANNIBAL (*moving toward the gong on the table*)

I'd better send for the Sergeant. You've lived long enough.

AMYTIS (*hastily*)

No, Hannibal—not yet. I'm not quite ready to die.

HANNIBAL

Are you afraid—you who know so much about truth?

AMYTIS

I don't want to die until I have lived. That's perfectly reasonable, isn't it?

HANNIBAL

I can give you death—but I can't give you life.

AMYTIS

How do you know you can't?

HANNIBAL

I don't know what it is. I don't want to know.

AMYTIS

I do want to know. I came here because I was determined to find out.

HANNIBAL

Mago was right, Amytis—you're dangerous.

AMYTIS

That's what they said of me in Rome. But it isn't so. I'm not dangerous. I'm only real.

HANNIBAL

You might be dangerous to me.

AMYTIS

Because you're afraid I might make *you* real.

HANNIBAL

You can't do it. No one can. When I was a child, my father laid me on the altar of Ba-al and consecrated me to the destruction of Rome. Since that moment, I've never been an individual

—I've been a force, divinely inspired to crush the enemies of Carthage.

AMYTIS

You're using the gods again—as an excuse for your own murders.

HANNIBAL

Those who kill for the glory of the gods are not murderers.

AMYTIS

Who told you that? One of the high-priests, I suppose.

HANNIBAL

Ba-al himself has spoken to me. Throughout my life I have been driven forward by his voice, saying, "Go on, Hannibal, go on, with sword and flame, until you have destroyed the glory of Rome."

AMYTIS

That wasn't the voice of Ba-al, Hannibal. That was the voice of the shopkeepers in Carthage, who are afraid that Rome will interfere with their trade. . . . Hatred, greed, envy, and the passionate desire for revenge—those are the high ideals that inspire you soldiers, Roman and Carthaginian alike . . . and when you realize the shameful futility of your great conquests, you turn around and attribute it all to the gods. . . . The gods are always convenient in an emergency . . .

HANNIBAL (*slightly nettled*)

What, may I ask, is the object of all this conversation? Do you think you can talk me away from Rome?

AMYTIS

I don't care *what* happens to Rome. I'm trying to find something in you, something great, something noble, something exciting.

HANNIBAL

And you expect to accomplish this by insulting me, by calling me a rotten murderer, blaspheming my gods.

AMYTIS

Good! You're getting angry at last. That's an encouraging sign!

HANNIBAL

I'm beginning to entertain an extreme dislike for you. If you'll forgive me for saying so, you're becoming something of a pest.

AMYTIS

I've tried to be interesting.

HANNIBAL

You've succeeded in being exceptionally irritating. I don't want to hear any more. You'll have to die.

AMYTIS

Right this minute?

HANNIBAL

Yes. I'll be glad to get it over with.

(*In the subsequent speeches,* AMYTIS *betrays*

*signs of tremulousness. Much of her amazing
assurance is gone.*)

AMYTIS

But isn't this very unusual?

HANNIBAL

The execution of an enemy?   No, I'm sorry to
say that it is entirely according to regulations.

AMYTIS

Oh, I know that.   But you ought not to kill me
at once, without—without——

HANNIBAL

Without what?   I've given you a meal, I've
answered your damned questions—what more can
I do?

AMYTIS

There's a certain—a certain ceremony to be
gone through with, isn't there?

HANNIBAL

What sort of a ceremony?

AMYTIS

But it—it's so embarrassing to put it into
words.

HANNIBAL

I'll count five.   If you can't find words in that
time, I'm afraid the subject—whatever it is—will
have to remain closed forever. . . . One. . . .
Two. . . . Three. . . . You'd better hurry. . . .
Four. . . .

AMYTIS

I can't say it, Hannibal. You'd better call the Sergeant.

(*There is a long pause, while* HANNIBAL *studies her expression of mute but eloquent desperation.*)

HANNIBAL

Oh! (*He backs away from her.*) Is *that* the ceremony you had in mind?

AMYTIS

But no soldier ever kills a woman until he . . . and es*pec*ially if she happens to be attractive.

HANNIBAL

You rather fancy yourself, don't you?

AMYTIS

Naturally, I shouldn't have come here at all if I had been lacking in a certain amount of self-confidence.

HANNIBAL

I'm sorry to disappoint you. I should have been delighted to justify your confidence if the circumstances had been more favorable for a—an event of this kind.

AMYTIS

More favorable! How could any circumstances be more favorable. Here you are—alone, in the night—with your triumphant army behind you, with Rome cringing at your feet. Here you are, Hannibal—and here am I!

(*He makes a step forward, toward her, and for*

a moment there is the suggestion that he has weakened.   But he braces himself, and again steps back.)

HANNIBAL

I'll have to decline your kind offer and put you to death . . . and this time you won't be allowed to talk your way out of it.

(*There is a piercing shriek off-stage at the left, followed by an incoherent rumble of gruff voices. META dashes in from the left. She is sobbing hysterically.   AMYTIS rushes to her and takes her in her arms, attempting to calm and comfort her.*)
What is it?   What's happened?

META (*wildly*)

Varius—save him . . .

AMYTIS (*to* HANNIBAL)

You gave me your word . . .

(*VARIUS rushes in, considerably dishevelled. He is followed by the SERGEANT and the FIRST and SECOND GUARDSMEN.*)

HANNIBAL

What is this, Sergeant?

SERGEANT

He started a fight, sir . . .

VARIUS (*breathlessly*)

One of the soldiers tried to attack her . . .

AMYTIS (*gasping with rage*)

What did he do?

META (*between sobs*)

He tried to carry me away with him . . .

VARIUS

I went after him, my lady . . .

AMYTIS

I hope you killed him.

VARIUS

I knocked him down.

META

Then I ran here . . .

AMYTIS

You poor darling.

VARIUS

Then they all went after me.

AMYTIS (*to* HANNIBAL)

Is this the way your men obey orders?

HANNIBAL (*to the* SERGEANT)

I told you that you were to be responsible . . .

(MAGO *breezes in.*)

MAGO (*briskly*)

What's all this?

AMYTIS (*flaming*)

You were the one. *You* attacked her—you
beast!

MAGO (*startled*)

Why, I did *not*. I . . .

AMYTIS

Don't try to lie out of it.   I know your licentious ways.

MAGO (*bewildered*)

Why—I don't even know what happened.   How could I . . .

AMYTIS

You'd have done the same thing to me if Hannibal hadn't stopped you.

MAGO (*to* HANNIBAL)

What *is* going on here, anyway?

HANNIBAL

I should like very much to know.   Sergeant, who attacked this girl?

AMYTIS

He did it.   I know he did it—the beast!

MAGO

I'm *not* a beast!

HANNIBAL

Never mind about that.   What happened, Sergeant?

AMYTIS

He's a disgrace to the army!

SERGEANT

It was one of Hasdrubal's men, sir.

MAGO

There!   Do you hear that?

SERGEANT

He crept up in the darkness, sir, when we wasn't looking, and tried to carry her off.

(META *breaks out with a fresh burst of sobs.*
AMYTIS *still holds her in her arms and comforts
her.*)

AMYTIS

There, there, dear—it's all right. He can't
touch you now. (*She looks at* MAGO *as she says
this.*)

MAGO

Will you please be quiet and listen to the Sergeant?

SERGEANT

This man (*referring to* VARIUS) went after her
before we knew what was up, and we figured we'd
better get him calmed down before he tried to
fight the whole army.

HANNIBAL

Where is the soldier who committed this indis-
cretion?

SERGEANT

He ain't woke up yet, sir.

AMYTIS

Good for you, Varius!

VARIUS

I lost my temper, my lady.

MAGO

Well—are you satisfied that it wasn't I?

AMYTIS

I wish it had been.

HANNIBAL

The soldier will be put to death, Sergeant.

MAGO

For a little thing like that?

HANNIBAL

It's not a little thing. Misconduct of this sort is not to be tolerated. There's been too much of it in our army. It's got to stop! (*As he says this, he glances meaningly at* AMYTIS.)

AMYTIS

You're quite right, Hannibal. That sort of thing ought to be discouraged.

HANNIBAL

You may go, Sergeant.

SERGEANT (*indicating* VARIUS *and* META)
And how about them, sir?

HANNIBAL

Take them with you.

SERGEANT

Come on.

META (*quailing*)

I—I'm afraid.

VARIUS

You mustn't be afraid, Meta. I won't leave you.

HANNIBAL

You'll wait for my orders, Sergeant. In the meantime, these prisoners are to be guarded more carefully. Do you understand?

SERGEANT

Yes, sir.

VARIUS

Come on, Meta.   (*He puts his arm about her and leads her out, followed by the* SERGEANT *and* GUARDSMEN.)

AMYTIS

If anyone so much as lays a finger on her, I— I'll . . .

MAGO

You'll do *what?*

AMYTIS

Oh—are you still here?

MAGO

Yes—but I'm going. And you're coming along with me. Isn't she, Hannibal?

HANNIBAL

Yes, you can take her out.

AMYTIS

Is it all over, Hannibal?   Am I going to die?

HANNIBAL

You're going to die.

MAGO

Come on.   (*He takes her toward the steps.*)

AMYTIS (*turning*)

You'll be sorry, Hannibal. (*She turns and is about to go down the steps.*)

HANNIBAL

Wait a minute, Mago.

MAGO

We mustn't delay any longer.

HANNIBAL

Bring her here.

MAGO

You haven't changed your mind?

HANNIBAL

Give me your sword. (MAGO *draws his sword, a long dagger, and hands it to* HANNIBAL.) I'm going to kill her myself. I'll send for you when it's over.

(*There is a shrill bugle call. Outside, the* COR-PORAL *is seen changing guard. When this is over, the* CORPORAL *stands by the curtains at the back, prepared to lower them.*)

MAGO (*crestfallen*)

Can't I stay and watch?

HANNIBAL

Go on, Mago.

MAGO (*to* AMYTIS)

It's an honor to die by the hand of Hannibal. Perhaps you deserve it. (*There is a note of admiration in his voice. He goes out. The* CORPO-RAL *lowers the curtains, and as he does so the lights are dimmed.* HANNIBAL *and* AMYTIS *face each other.*)

HANNIBAL

You've called me a murderer. You say that I glory in my reputation for cruelty. Now I'm go-

ing to justify that reputation. I shall give you
the final satisfaction of knowing that Hannibal,
the merciless conqueror of Rome, is not a myth.
. . . Come here . . .

(*She advances to him, slowly but without hesi-
tation. He clutches her throat with his left hand.
His right hand holds the dagger.*)

AMYTIS

Why do you choose to have me die, this way?

HANNIBAL

I couldn't trust Mago to do this. You might
have told him some of the things you have told me.
He might have weakened.

AMYTIS

Yes—Mago is a man. You, of course, are a
god. . . . Perhaps some day you'll discover that
you're a man, too, Hannibal—and not ashamed
to weaken. . . . Perhaps, some day, you'll realize
that there's a thing called the human equation.
It's so much more beautiful than war.

HANNIBAL

The human equation does not interest me.

AMYTIS

Because you don't know what it is. If you
could ever find it, you'd know that all your conquests—all your glory—are only whispers in the
infinite stillness of time—that Rome is no more
than a tiny speck on the face of eternity—that
the gods are the false images of the unimagina-

tive . . . and then you'll wish that all that you've done could be undone.

HANNIBAL

Where can I go to find this human equation?

AMYTIS

It is here—on earth—not on the heights of Olympus.

HANNIBAL

Perhaps I'll find it—but never with you. You must die. (*He is very close to her.*)

AMYTIS

War is death, Hannibal. Rome is dying, Carthage is dying—but we're alive. . . . You can conquer men, Hannibal. You can conquer armies. But you can't conquer life.

HANNIBAL

You must die.

AMYTIS

Go out and destroy the wind, Hannibal. Destroy the stars, and the night itself—if you can. Then come back and kill me.

(*A bugle is heard, blowing the Carthaginian version of "taps"—softly, slowly.*)

(HANNIBAL, *using all his strength, tries to thrust her away from him and lifts the dagger higher, preparing to plunge it in her heart. She clings desperately to his arms.*)

HANNIBAL (*his voice now tremulous*)

You're going to die!

AMYTIS

Yes—I'm going to die . . . but not until to-morrow. . . . (*Her face is close to his—too close. He kisses her.*)

(*Presently*, AMYTIS *draws away from him and gazes, unsmilingly, into his eyes.* HANNIBAL *raises the sword, thinks better of it, and throws the sword away, vehemently. Again he seizes her in his arms and kisses her.*)

CURTAIN.

ACT III

ACT III

(*The Scene is the same as* ACT II—*the time, early the following morning.*)

(*There is a roll of drums as the curtain rises.* MAHARBAL, CARTHALO, *and* HASDRUBAL *are grouped around the table, in conference. The* SERGEANT *and the* FIRST *and* SECOND GUARDSMEN *are at the back.*)

MAHARBAL

Wouldn't it be wise to assemble some siege machinery before we start?

HASDRUBAL

Machinery be damned! The Romans know they're beaten already—that's the main thing. We don't need machinery to break down resistance that doesn't exist.

CARTHALO

The Roman walls are thick. We'll need battering rams at least.

HASDRUBAL

I suppose you think you know more about it than Hannibal does. If he wanted any battering rams, he'd make 'em.

MAHARBAL

Then it will be up to the infantry to storm the walls.

HASDRUBAL

You won't need the infantry after I've attacked.

CARTHALO

Our infantry has the right to occupy the city first.   We've earned that privilege.

(HANNIBAL *enters from the left and stands behind the column, so that he is unseen by the others.*)

MAHARBAL (*hotly*)

How about my men?   Do you think we're going to follow the cavalry in?

HASDRUBAL (*even more hotly*)

What are you talking about?   The Numidian cavalry corps is going in first, and by the gods . . .

CARTHALO (*cutting in*)

They will not!   The infantry has done all the heavy work in this war . . .

HASDRUBAL (*cutting in*)

The heavy work, eh!   Who did the heavy work at Trasimenus—who did the heavy work at Cannæ—who . . .

MAHARBAL (*cutting in*)

The infantry, not the cavalry.   We deserve to go into Rome first.

CARTHALO

Of course we do.   You always want all the honors for your damned cavalry.

(HANNIBAL *steps from behind the column.*)

SERGEANT

'Tshun! (*He and the three officers salute.*)

CARTHALO

You can settle this, sir.

HANNIBAL

Settle what?

HASDRUBAL

It's these damned infantry officers, sir. They think they're going to occupy the city first. The infantry!

MAHARBAL

It's the infantry's job. The cavalry is only supposed——

CARTHALO

And besides, my men can be trusted to do it right. They——

HANNIBAL

I think this can be settled without bloodshed.

HASDRUBAL

The cavalry goes in first.

MAHARBAL

The infantry won't stand for it.

HANNIBAL

We'll do it this way. You'll attack the city from the west, Hasdrubal. You attack from the south, Carthalo, and you from the north, Maharbal. We can send Mago against the east gate. All the Romans will concentrate there, to watch the elephants. The rest of you will break in easily.

CARTHALO

But which of us is to go in first?

HANNIBAL

You can all start at the same time—and the first one to reach the Forum—will win a prize.

HASDRUBAL

What is the prize?

HANNIBAL

I'll have to decide about that later. In the meantime, you can fall your men in.

MAHARBAL

Yes, sir.

HANNIBAL

Wait for further orders.

CARTHALO

Yes, sir.

(*The three of them salute and go out.*)

HASDRUBAL (*as they go*)

The cavalry will go in first!

CARTHALO

Not by a damned sight . . .

MAHARBAL

We'll see who wins that prize . . .

(*They are all talking at once as they disappear from view.*)

HANNIBAL

Pack up this equipment, Sergeant.

SERGEANT

Yes, sir! Get busy, you!

(*The* FIRST *and* SECOND GUARDSMEN *start to pack up the maps, armor, etc., placing them in a large chest, which they carry out.*)

HANNIBAL

Have your men ready in half an hour.

(BALA *comes in bearing a tray of food, which he deposits on the table.*)

SERGEANT

Full marching order, sir?

HANNIBAL

No. Put their packs on the wagon.

SERGEANT

Yes, sir. (*He salutes and goes out.*)

HANNIBAL

Get your kitchen packed up, Bala. Then come back here and get my things. (BALA *bows and starts.*) And Bala . . . send those Roman slaves in to me.

(BALA *goes out.* HANNIBAL *is standing by the table, eating bread and drinking wine, this being his hasty breakfast. The change in his manner must be apparent: he is now gay, buoyant, carefree, and reluctant to concentrate on the serious business at hand. He has the air of one who doesn't much care whether school keeps or not. He glances toward the left.* VARIUS *and* META *come in, hesitantly. Their hands are tightly clasped, as though they are clinging to each other in the face of a common danger.*)

VARIUS

You sent for us, sir?

HANNIBAL

Yes! You're wanted in there. (*He nods toward the left.* VARIUS *and* META *go out.*)

(*During this, and subsequent scenes, there is almost constant movement outside the temple. The* GUARDSMEN *pass to and fro, hurriedly, carrying equipment of various kinds. There must be the sense of intensive action—of rapid but systematic preparation for the battle that is imminent.*)

(MAGO *comes in quietly at the back, leans against one of the pillars, folds his arms, and looks at* HANNIBAL, *who is still standing, hastily gulping his breakfast.* MAGO *is attired in a shiny new uniform.*)

MAGO

Well . . .?

HANNIBAL (*turns and sees* MAGO)
Oh, hello—Mago.

MAGO

You're a *fine* example, you are. (*He comes down stage.*) What have you got to say for yourself now?

HANNIBAL

Nothing, Mago. It would take years to explain this.

MAGO

You're darned right it would.

HANNIBAL

What did you think had happened last night?

MAGO (*indignantly*)

What did I think had happened! What else *could* I think? I stood out there, for hour after hour, waiting for you to send for me.

HANNIBAL

You shouldn't have waited.

MAGO

When I finally looked in here, the room was empty. . . . Even my own supper was all eaten up.

HANNIBAL (*with a glance toward the left*)

She ate it.

MAGO

Of all the damned outrages!

HANNIBAL

You can eat breakfast here, if you want, to make up for the supper you missed. The army moves in half an hour.

MAGO

The elephants are ready.

HANNIBAL

And incidentally—perhaps it would be just as well if . . .

MAGO

Oh, don't worry about that. I won't say a word.

HANNIBAL (*laughing*)

Thanks.

MAGO

I can't understand it, Hannibal. It's the first serious mistake you've ever made.

HANNIBAL

I've made many mistakes, Mago—but this isn't one of them. (*He goes out, munching an apple.*)
(*A bugle call is heard.*)

(*MAGO sits down at the table and starts to eat. He chuckles to himself. AMYTIS comes in through the door at the left. She is wearing the Phœnician nightgown, and a brilliant blue cloak. She passes behind the column, going to the right to gaze out after HANNIBAL. MAGO has not seen her. She turns to him.*)

AMYTIS

Good *morning*.
(*MAGO starts.*)

MAGO (*with no enthusiasm*)

Oh! Good morning.

AMYTIS

Having breakfast?
(*AMYTIS is also a changed person. There are*

*no evidences of her cheerful flippancy. She is
langourous, meditative, reserved.*)

MAGO

Yes. . . . Can't I persuade *you* to have a little
something to eat?

AMYTIS

Thanks, I will. (*She sits down at the table with*
MAGO *and joins in the repast.*) What were you
laughing at when I came in?

MAGO

I was just thinking what Rome will look like to-
night, after we've finished with it.

(*Another bugle call is heard.*)

AMYTIS

There'll be nothing left, will there?

MAGO (*finishing a mouthful*)

Nothing. First, we'll slaughter the men. When
we've got them out of the way, we'll start plun-
dering and see what we can pick up in the way
of loot. After that, we'll set fire to the houses.
. . . And then . . .

AMYTIS

Oh, I know what comes next.

MAGO

Exactly. After we've disposed of everything
else, we'll turn to the women. . . . Are there any
attractive women in Rome

AMYTIS (*after a moment's thought*)

Oh—any number of them. A trifle unimaginative, perhaps—but still, attractive.

MAGO

Do you think they'll be attracted to me?

AMYTIS

I don't quite see how they can avoid it. After all . . .

MAGO

Oh, I know what you mean. You mean, they won't dare refuse.

AMYTIS

That's about it, isn't it?

MAGO

Personally, I don't like that sort of thing—force, I mean. I like to feel that it's sort of—sort of mutual. Do you understand?

AMYTIS

I do, indeed.

MAGO

I mean to say—I like to think that they're giving in cheerfully.

AMYTIS

There's no question of that. You look magnificent in that gorgeous new uniform.

MAGO

Do you really think so? As a matter of fact, I've been saving that up for the entry into Rome. (*He stands up and draws himself to his full height.*)   Today, the women of Rome will feast their eyes on a real Carthaginian soldier.

AMYTIS

I'm sure that the women of Rome will be duly appreciative.

MAGO (*sitting down again*)

Hannibal will probably make me change back to my old uniform.   He's always telling me not to show off.

AMYTIS

Tonight, when you run wild in Rome, will Hannibal join in the general merriment?

MAGO

If you'll allow me to say so, I think Hannibal has started that already.

(*The* SERGEANT *comes in quickly and salutes.*)

SERGEANT

Beg pardon, sir.

MAGO

What is it?

SERGEANT

Some Romans, sir.

(MAGO *springs up.*)

MAGO

Some *Romans?*   Attacking?

SERGEANT

No, sir.   It's a delegation of 'em, under a flag of truce.

MAGO

Send for Hannibal, quick! He's down con-
ferring with Hasdrubal.

SERGEANT

Yes, sir. (*He goes to the back and calls out to
the* THIRD GUARDSMAN.) Hey, you! (*The* THIRD
GUARDSMAN *appears.*) Run down to Hasdrubal's
tent and tell the commander-in-chief that there's
a delegation of Romans here--and make it fast!
(*The* THIRD GUARDSMAN *dashes off.*)

MAGO (*turning to* AMYTIS)

Do you know anything about this?

AMYTIS

I haven't the fainest idea what . . .

MAGO

It's some damned trick, and you're part of it.
Are they armed, Sergeant?

SERGEANT

Oh, no, sir. We went all over 'em, carefully.

MAGO

What did they say?

SERGEANT

They just said they'd like to see the commander-in-chief

MAGO

Did you get their names?

SERGEANT

Only the leader—said his name was Fabius
Maximus.

AMYTIS (*terrified*)

My husband! (*She jumps up.*)

MAGO

A—ha! So you *do* know something?

AMYTIS

I've got to get out of here. (*She hurries toward the left.*)

MAGO

You'd better not try to communicate with your husband.

AMYTIS (*hastily*)

Don't worry. I won't. (*She goes out through the door. MAHARBAL appears at the back.*)

MAGO (*muttering*)

Damn her soul. I'd like to . . .

(MAHARBAL *comes in.*)

MAHARBAL

What do you suppose they want?

MAGO

I don't know. It looks pretty suspicious.

MAHARBAL

They'd better not try any of their tricks on Hannibal.

SERGEANT

Shall I bring 'em, sir?

MAHARBAL

Yes, bring them in.

(BALA *unobtrusively removes the breakfast tray and goes out.*)

CARTHALO (*entering*)

The runner just told me.

MAHARBAL

Is Hannibal coming?

CARTHALO

Yes.

MAGO

I tell you, Maharbal, we'll have to stand by Hannibal now.

MAHARBAL

Nonsense. This doesn't mean anything. These Romans are just making a last desperate attempt to save themselves.

CARTHALO

It's their only hope.

MAGO (*desperately*)

But I tell you, Hannibal is not himself. . . . He . . .

MAHARBAL (*reassuringly*)

Calm down, Mago, calm down. It'll be *all* right. Hannibal is still Hannibal.

(*The* SERGEANT *appears. There is a roll of drums, which continues until* HANNIBAL'S *entrance.*)

SERGEANT

This way . . .

(FABIUS *enters, followed by* SCIPIO, DRUSUS, *the* CORPORAL, *and four* GUARDSMEN. *The Romans salute; the Carthaginians return the greet-*

ing. The GUARDSMEN, *with swords drawn, take
up positions by the columns at the back, remaining there, rigidly at attention, throughout the ensuing scene.*)

(FABIUS *is obviously nervous, moving as one
who expects to be stabbed in the back at any moment. He looks apprehensively toward* MAGO,
MAHARBAL, *and* CARTHALO, *who are at the right.*
SCIPIO *also regards them, but there is a belligerent flash in his eye. He had objected strenuously
to this attempt at compromise, and during the
parley he shows his impatience and dissatisfaction
with the whole proceeding.*)

FABIUS (*clearing his throat*)

Which of you is Hannibal?

CARTHALO

Hannibal will be here directly.

MAHARBAL

You're wasting your time, Romans. You'd better go back and defend your city.

SCIPIO

Do you hear that, Fabius? He's right!

DRUSUS

Hush, Scipio! Let Fabius do the talking.

SERGEANT

'Tshun!

SCIPIO

There he is!

(HANNIBAL *enters, followed by* HASDRUBAL.

The Carthaginians and Romans salute, sharply.
Hannibal, *very erect and very serious, confronts
his enemies.*)

HANNIBAL

Which one of you is Fabius Maximus?

FABIUS (*pleased*)

I am.

HASDRUBAL (*barking*)

When you speak to Hannibal, say "Sir"!

HANNIBAL (*gazing intently at* FABIUS)

So you're Fabius Maximus. . . . That explains
a great deal. (*He sits down at the table. The
others remain standing.*)

HASDRUBAL

Come on, speak up! What do you want?

FABIUS

We came here under a flag of truce, sir. We
felt that we might talk this over in a civilized
manner.

HANNIBAL

I can see no objection to that.

FABIUS (*getting over his first nervousness*)

Here you are, Hannibal, at the gates of Rome,
with a mighty army—an admirable army. Even
though we are your enemies, we'll cheerfully admit
that.

HASDRUBAL

Never mind the soft soap.   What do you want?

FABIUS (*expanding*)

For years, Rome and Carthage have been at each other's throats, in a death struggle, gentlemen, a death struggle. Thousands upon thousands of men—on *both* sides—have sacrificed their lives. It has all been most unfortunate. Just at present, the conflict seems to have reached what I may reasonably call a crisis.

HANNIBAL

You are not overstating it.

FABIUS

As I have already pointed out, here you stand at the gates of Rome, confronting our army, which is of sufficient strength to defend the city for months.

HASDRUBAL

That's a damned lie. You couldn't hold out for an hour.

HANNIBAL

Never mind that, Hasdrubal. . . . Go on . . .

FABIUS

You may not realize the full strength of our defending force. We now have, within the city, twenty war-strength legions, fully armed and prepared . . .

HASDRUBAL

Don't listen to him, Hannibal. Twenty legions! Do you expect us to believe that? Why, you have two legions, at the outside, and home guard at that. There's not a man in 'em who isn't a great-grandfather, at least.

HANNIBAL

Keep quiet, Hasdrubal. I'll hold up our end of the conversation. . . . Now, what else have you to offer?

FABIUS

I need not enlarge upon the physical advantages of our position. You must know that the walls of Rome are practically impregnable.

HANNIBAL

Well?

FABIUS

Well, then—what will be gained by a long, arduous, painful siege? Nothing, my dear sir, but acute suffering on both sides. We will sacrifice the lives of many gallant young soldiers, and so will you. And at the same time, there are the innocent victims to be thought of—the women, and the little children. What of them? This is not their war, Hannibal. They didn't start it. They have no axe to grind with you. . . . Why must they be made to pay the terrible price of pitched battle?

HANNIBAL

What do you suggest we do about all this?

FABIUS

I suggest that you abandon the idea of captur-

ing Rome.   The attempt would cost you heavily
and would be doomed to ultimate failure.

HASDRUBAL

In other words, we're to lay down our arms and
go home.   (*He laughs heartily.*)

FABIUS

Oh, no—not exactly that.   We realize that the
war must be brought to a logical conclusion.   But
we do suggest that you move to some spot, not
quite so near the city, where we can meet you hon-
orably on the field of battle.

HASDRUBAL

How about those twenty legions of yours?
Why don't you send them out here and let us fight
it out?

FABIUS

We shall be glad to do that, in due time.

HASDRUBAL

Do you hear that?   In due time!   He wants us
to wait until he can get his armies back from
Capua and Spain.   (HASDRUBAL, MAHARBAL, *and*
CARTHALO *laugh.*)

HANNIBAL

Have you any further suggestions?

FABIUS

No—I think that's about all.

HASDRUBAL

Well, it isn't enough.   If you think you can
beg us off with a few hollow words, you're damned

well mistaken. Our army is mobilized at this minute—forty thousand men, waiting for the order to move. Within an hour we'll have surrounded Rome—and then we'll see what sort of defense your twenty legions can put up.

SCIPIO (*bursting at this*)

Twenty legions or not—we'll show you that we can fight better than we can talk!

DRUSUS

Keep out of this, Scipio. Leave it to Fabius.

SCIPIO

I can't keep out of it. I've fought against you, Hannibal, at Trasimenus and Cannæ, and by the gods, I'll fight against you again!

FABIUS

Scipio—*please!*

SCIPIO

Hasdrubal is right. We can't stand them off with hollow words. We never should have come out here in the first place. Let them come to us.

DRUSUS

Hold your tongue, Scipio. You'll spoil everything.

HANNIBAL

I seem to detect a slight note of dissension.

FABIUS

Oh, no—not at all. Scipio just felt that it was unwise for us to talk this over with you . . .

HASDRUBAL

Scipio seems to be a real soldier. It's too bad you haven't more of them in Rome.

SCIPIO (*to* FABIUS)

I told you not to listen to that damned woman. She put the idea into your head.

HANNIBAL (*interested*)

What damned woman?

FABIUS

It was just a personal matter, I assure you.

SCIPIO

She was the one who suggested it.

HANNIBAL

Who was?

FABIUS

As a matter of fact, sir, it was my wife.

HANNIBAL

Oh! Your wife!

MAGO

I thought so. It was his *wife!*

HANNIBAL

Keep quiet, Mago.

FABIUS

She had the idea that you might consider this matter reasonably . . .

SCIPIO

She's a cowardly Greek, herself, and she succeeded in converting Fabius to her point of view.

HANNIBAL

Fabius must be a model husband. . . . But, after all, these domestic affairs are not of vital importance to us at the moment.

HASDRUBAL

You're damned right they aren't. Send these men back, Hannibal. The army is ready to attack. We can't wait.

HANNIBAL

We'll have to wait. I want time to think some things over.

HASDRUBAL

You don't have to give this a second thought— why, it's ridiculous on the face of it.

HANNIBAL

Nevertheless, I intend to think it over. . . . Mago, take these gentlemen down and show them the elephants. They might be interested.

FABIUS (*apprehensively*)

You're not going to violate the flag of truce?

HANNIBAL

No—no. You'll be as safe here as you are in Rome . . . safer.

MAGO (*reluctantly*)

Come on. (*He leads the three Romans out. They are followed by the* CORPORAL *and the* THREE GUARDSMEN.)

HANNIBAL (*to the other officers*)

You gentlemen get back to your units. Be ready to move at a moment's notice.

HASDRUBAL

You're not going to be taken in by what those damned Romans said, are you? You can't delay the destruction of Rome another day. It would mean mutiny . . .

HANNIBAL

You heard your orders. (HASDRUBAL, MAHARBAL, *and* CARTHALO *go out. Three bugle calls are heard.*) You can wait outside, Sergeant.

(*The* SERGEANT *goes out.* AMYTIS *comes in.*)

AMYTIS

Don't believe a word of it, Hannibal. They haven't twenty legions in the city, or anything like it.

HANNIBAL

I know all that.

AMYTIS

Poor Fabius. I can just picture him brooding over that suggestion of mine. I made it quite casually. He probably worried about it all night, trying to persuade himself and Scipio and the others that I was right.

HANNIBAL

Why did you make that suggestion? Why did you think I'd listen to reason?

AMYTIS

I don't know. Why did I think so last night, for that matter?

HANNIBAL

You seem to guess right most of the time.

AMYTIS

I have one more favor to ask, Hannibal.

HANNIBAL

Is it as reasonable as the first one?

AMYTIS

It's about my slaves—I want them to go back to their homes—to be free. Will you take them with you?

HANNIBAL

Where do they come from?

AMYTIS

From Sicily.

HANNIBAL

I can send them there.

(AMYTIS *goes to the left and summons* VARIUS *and* META, *who come in at once.*)

AMYTIS

Hannibal is going to send you to Sicily. You're to be free.

META

Free—to go home?

VARIUS

And to be married?

AMYTIS

You'll be free to do anything you please.

HANNIBAL

You'll find Bala outside.

META

Good-bye, my lady——and thank you.

VARIUS

May the gods bless you for being good to us.

AMYTIS

Be good to each other——and forget that you were ever slaves in Rome.

META

We shall never forget you, my lady——or your kindness.

AMYTIS

Good-bye, both of you. I want you to be happy. (*They go out.*) I'm glad they're to be saved.

HANNIBAL

You too can be saved, Amytis——if you choose.

AMYTIS

If I choose?

HANNIBAL

Did you hear my conversation with your husband?

AMYTIS

Yes——I heard it all.

HANNIBAL

I delayed my decision——because I wanted to give you your choice. Last night, I should have put you to death. I shouldn't have listened to a word of protest or persuasion. But I did listen——and you didn't die. . . . This morning, it is different.

. . . I can't destroy Rome until I know what your choice is to be. . . . I will spare your husband's life. You can go back to him, and I'll see that you both are allowed to escape—to go wherever you please . . . that's one part of your choice, Amytis.

AMYTIS

And the other part?

HANNIBAL

To go with me. To forget Rome—to forget Carthage—to be with me, forever . . .

AMYTIS

And if I agree to that part of it, will Rome be spared?

HANNIBAL (*emphatically*)

No! Whatever your choice, Rome must be destroyed!

AMYTIS

Then I choose to go back to my husband. . . . Go ahead with your great work, Hannibal. Burn Rome to the ground; obliterate it. Keep your army here forever, to make sure Rome stays destroyed. Instruct your men to crush any blade of grass, any flower that dares to thrust its head above the ashes of the dead city. Prolong your victory. Glory in it till your dying day. . . . But don't ever look to me, or to my memory, for sympathy or applause.

HANNIBAL (*angrily*)

I think I understand you at last. You came here to save Rome. If you fail in that, you're prepared to die. For all your talk, you care nothing for me.

AMYTIS

You mustn't believe that, Hannibal.

(*There is a shrill bugle call.*)

HANNIBAL

You thought you could save Rome from the destiny that is ready to overwhelm it! You have tried to build walls of words as a defense against my army.

AMYTIS

I'm not trying to save Rome, Hannibal. I'm trying to save you.

HANNIBAL

Why do you imagine that I'm worth saving?

AMYTIS

Because I want to have you—always—as my possession. Let Rome and Carthage remember you as a great general. I want to remember you as a conqueror who could realize the glory of submission.

HANNIBAL (*challenging*)

And does Rome realize the glory of submission?

AMYTIS

No, and for that very reason Rome will destroy itself. Success is like a strong wine, Hannibal;

give a man enough of it, and he'll drink himself to death. Rome will do that, too, if you leave it alone.

HANNIBAL

So I'm to leave Rome—and to leave you. Is that your choice?

AMYTIS

Yes, Hannibal—to leave me with something beautiful—something that is worth remembering. I don't want you to spoil that.

HANNIBAL

And what shall I have to remember? That I marched three thousand miles—and failed.

AMYTIS

Ah, but that's just the point, Hannibal. You haven't failed.

HANNIBAL

I came to conquer Rome. Anything short of that is failure.

AMYTIS

Are you sure of that? Are you sure that you didn't come all this way to find your own soul?

HANNIBAL

My own soul doesn't matter, Amytis. I myself amount to nothing. All of us amount to nothing. . . . We stand aside and watch ourselves parade by! We're proud of the brave manner in which we step forward, and of the nobility of our bearing, and the sparkle of divine fire that is in our eyes—and actually we have no more idea of where we're going, no more choice in the matter, than so many drops of water in a flowing river.

AMYTIS

Yes, and at the end of that river is an endless sea of things that are passed. It is called history. When you reach that sea, other drops of water may murmur respectfully, "Here comes Hannibal, the conqueror of Rome." But you won't care. You'll only be thankful for the interludes that you have known—the moments when you drifted from the main current and found peace and contentment in the deep, quiet pools.

(They are standing close together, facing each other. With sudden, fierce strength, HANNIBAL takes her in his arms.)

HANNIBAL

I'll turn away from Rome now, Amytis, if you'll come with me. . . . Rome can live, Amytis. You can save it . . .

AMYTIS

I don't want it to be that way . . .

HANNIBAL

I'll bury my sword before the gates of Rome. I'll hand over my command to Hasdrubal. I'll do the one thing I thought was impossible: I'll quit when I'm winning. But I can't do this alone . . . I can't . . .

AMYTIS

No, Hannibal. I don't want it to be that way.
I don't want Rome to be saved because I made
this choice . . . I want you to do it—to make
the decision—to prove that you are stronger than
your own victorious army . . .

HANNIBAL

If I recognize your truths, I'll have to believe
that all my life has been wasted—that all those
men who have fallen along the road to Rome have
died for nothing. Do you want me to believe that?

AMYTIS

I do! I do! I want you to believe that every
sacrifice made in the name of war is wasted.
When you believe that, you'll be a great man.
(*Gently, she strokes his hair.*)   I want you to be
a great man.

(*He kisses her, desperately.*)

MAGO (*offstage*)

Hannibal!   (MAGO *comes in, sees them embraced, and turns away.*)

(HANNIBAL *slowly relinquishes his grip on* AMY-
TIS *and steps back.*)

HANNIBAL

You were right, Mago. I should have let you
put her to death without further delay.

MAGO

I'm glad you realize that at last. You see—
I've had a lot more experience in these matters
than you've had. I understand the risks.

HANNIBAL

Evidently.

MAGO

It isn't too late to punish her, even now.

(HANNIBAL *crosses to the table.*)

HANNIBAL

Perhaps it isn't too late.   (*He beats the gong.*)

MAGO

The Romans are waiting for your decision.

(BALA *enters.*)

HANNIBAL

Send Thothmes here.

(BALA *bows and goes out.*)

MAGO

And the Romans?

HANNIBAL

Bring them here to me.

MAGO

Yes, sir.   (*He goes out.*)

AMYTIS

I must go.   My husband mustn't find me here
—he—he'd die of shame.

(*The* FIRST *and* SECOND GUARDSMEN *enter,
taking positions at either side of the main entrance.*)

HANNIBAL

Put that woman under arrest.

(*The two* GUARDSMEN *take her arms and hold
her.   She is at the left, upstage.*)

(THOTHMES *comes in.*)

AMYTIS

Hannibal—you can't do this. . . . Let me go!

THOTHMES

You sent for me, sir.

HANNIBAL

Have you your records with you?

THOTHMES

Yes, sir.   They're all here.

(MAGO *comes in, followed by the* CORPORAL, *three* GUARDSMEN, *and the three Romans. As* FABIUS *enters,* AMYTIS *shrinks back, so that he does not see her at first.*)

HANNIBAL

Did you see the elephants?

FABIUS

Oh, yes, indeed.   It was quite a treat.

DRUSUS

We don't see elephants around here very often.

(FABIUS *sees* AMYTIS.)

FABIUS

Amytis!   (*He starts toward her, but the* CORPORAL *stops him.*)   In the name of all the gods, what are you doing here?

AMYTIS

Fabius!   I didn't want you to . . .

HANNIBAL (*harshly*)

Our sentries arrested this woman.   She represented herself as your wife.

FABIUS

She is my wife! Amytis, why did you come here?

HANNIBAL

She told me that she was concerned for your safety. She came to find you.

FABIUS

Amytis! My true, my loyal wife. Do you hear that, Scipio, she came to find *me!*

AMYTIS

I can't let you believe . . .

HANNIBAL (*quickly*)

She evidently told us the truth. There is no reason why we should suspect the wife of Fabius Maximus. You may release her.

(*The* GUARDSMEN *release* AMYTIS *and she goes to* FABIUS' *side, standing before the column, where she remains until the end.*)

(HASDRUBAL, MAHARBAL, *and* CARTHALO *come in briskly, followed by the* SERGEANT.)

HASDRUBAL

The army is ready to attack.

HANNIBAL (*to* FABIUS)

I'm issuing an order in which you may be interested.

FABIUS (*tremulously*)

You're not going to . . .

HANNIBAL

The Carthaginian army will proceed at once to Capua.

HASDRUBAL (*wildly*)

We're not going into Rome?

HANNIBAL

No—we are not.

HASDRUBAL

What in the name of all the gods is the matter with you? Have you lost every atom of judgment?

HANNIBAL

I've lost nothing, Hasdrubal—except a few perverted notions about various things. I could afford to lose those.

HASDRUBAL

I won't stand for it. Do you hear that? I won't stand for it! You can take your goddamned army to Capua. My cavalry will attack Rome this morning——

MAHARBAL

I'll go with you, Hasdrubal.

CARTHALO

So will I.

HASDRUBAL

There! Do you hear that? The two finest officers in your army. They know what it would mean to turn back now. They haven't lost control of their senses.

MAHARBAL (*angrily*)

The trouble with you, sir, is that you know how to gain victories but not how to use them . . .

CARTHALO

Hasdrubal is absolutely right, sir. You'd better do as he says . . .

(*Both men are speaking at the same time, so
that there is a jumble of angry voices.*)

FABIUS

Gentlemen—gentlemen! Might I say a word?

HASDRUBAL

Shut up!

HANNIBAL

So you propose to destroy Rome by yourselves?

HASDRUBAL

We do—and by the gods, we'll take you with
us. You've led us all this way. And you'll see
it through, if we have to force you into it at the
point of a sword.

(HASDRUBAL *draws his sword and confronts*
HANNIBAL.)

HANNIBAL (*quietly, but with tremendous em-
phasis*)

Hasdrubal—you'll do as I say.

(HASDRUBAL *steps back a pace.*)

HASDRUBAL (*hoarsely*)

We can't do it, Hannibal. Even if we gave the
orders, the men wouldn't move away from Rome
now. After four years of steady fighting, they
won't be cheated out of their reward.

HANNIBAL

You and Maharbal and Carthalo and all the

others in this army have the misfortune to be soldiers. You can't break away from the habit of
obedience. You'll do as I say.

HASDRUBAL

Don't put that order through, Hannibal.
Don't—*don't!* It'll be the end of all of us—of
Carthage itself—and a rotten, humiliating end,
too.

HANNIBAL

The army moves to Capua at once. Go tell
your men to fall in.

HASDRUBAL

I've never disobeyed an order, Hannibal.
What's more, when you've given me a command,
I've never even stopped to ask why you gave it.
I've accepted everything from you, as though it
were the word of Ba-al himself. . . . But this is
different. I won't move from this spot until you
tell me why we are turning away from Rome.

HANNIBAL (*vaguely*)

Everyone seems to be so damned curious about
my motives.

HASDRUBAL

You owe that much to me—to every man in this
sweating army. Tell us why—why?

(HANNIBAL, *suddenly collected, steps forward
toward* HASDRUBAL.)

HANNIBAL

I'll tell you why, Hasdrubal . . . I've had a
portent. (*He says this mysteriously.*)

HASDRUBAL (*awed*)

A portent?

CARTHALO (*even more awed*)

From the gods?

HANNIBAL

Yes—a portent from the gods.

MAHARBAL

From Ba-al?

HANNIBAL

No—from Tanit, the daughter of Ba-al. (*This last with a furtive glance toward* AMYTIS.)

HASDRUBAL

Then there is no hope. If Ba-al has sent his daughter to rule our destiny, then we are lost, forever.

HANNIBAL (*speaking now directly at* AMYTIS, *as though they again were alone*)

She told me to look for the human equation. . . . When you have found that, she said, you will know that all your conquests, all your glory, are but whispers in the infinite stillness of time—that Rome is only a speck on the face of eternity.

CARTHALO

The gods speak strangely.

HANNIBAL

She told me that I must realize the glory of submission . . . I could only obey.

HASDRUBAL

The gods are cruel.

Hannibal

Cruel—but convenient, in an emergency. . . .
(Amytis *smiles tenderly.*) . . . We're going to
Capua—to rest. We need rest, more than we
need Rome. . . . Get to your posts!

(Hasdrubal *steps forward and confronts* Fabius, *menacingly.*)

Hasdrubal

The Carthaginian army retreats, for the first
time. But don't try to take credit for that, you
Romans! Don't ever forget that it was only the
gods themselves who saved Rome from the
strength of our swords. (*He turns, salutes* Hannibal, *and strides out, followed by* Maharbal *and*
Carthalo.)

(Mago *ambles in a leisurely manner across the
stage and faces* Amytis.)

Mago

So Hannibal had a portent, did he? (*He turns
to* Hannibal.) That's a new name for it. (*He
salutes and goes out.*)

Hannibal

Fall in the guard, Sergeant.

Sergeant

Yes, sir. Hup!

(*The* Sergeant, Corporal, *and* Guardsmen
march out.)

Hannibal (*to* Thothmes)

Give me your records, Thothmes. (Thothmes

hands him the records.) You may go. (THOTH-
MES *goes out. Three bugles are heard.* HANNI-
BAL *looks through the sheets of papyrus, and then
turns to the Romans.*) I have here a complete
record of our march, from Carthage to the gates
of Rome. I need hardly explain to you that this
is a document of great historical importance.
That being the case . . . (*He tears the sheets
into small pieces.*) It is now no longer a document of any importance whatever. The exploits of
Hannibal's magnificent army will live only as long
as our own memory survives. That's the end of
the story, gentlemen.

FABIUS

Hannibal—you've destroyed a chapter of History.

HANNIBAL

What difference does it make? In the end,
there'll be more than enough history to go 'round.

SCIPIO

I have seen you before, Hannibal—in battle.
Gods or no gods—it is not like you to do this—
to retreat.

HANNIBAL

I'm leaving Rome to an enemy that is crueller
even than I am. . . . I shall allow Rome to destroy itself.

SCIPIO

Perhaps we'll have the chance to fight it out
some day.

HANNIBAL (*bowing*)

I'm afraid so. (*He walks slowly to the back, then turns.*)

HANNIBAL

Fabius, I wish happiness and prosperity to you, your wife, and your sons.

FABIUS

Thank you—but I have no sons.

HANNIBAL

You may have . . . and if you do, I hope that your first-born will inherit the qualities of greatness that were so evident in his father—that he will duplicate his father's signal triumphs and that he, too, will ultimately discover the human equation. . . . (*He turns to* AMYTIS.) It is so much more beautiful than war.

AMYTIS (*in a whisper*)

Hannibal! You're a great man.

(*He takes an indecisive step toward her, as she stands before the column; the impulse, however, is only momentary. He steps back.*)

HANNIBAL

Good-bye, gentlemen. I wish you luck with your conquest of the world. (*He goes out.*)

(BALA *comes in from the left, picks up* HANNIBAL's *shield, and follows his master out. There is a shrill bugle call.*) FABIUS

What was all that he said about "the human equation"?

(DRUSUS *goes down the steps at the right,
standing at the back—still visible—and gazing
out after* HANNIBAL.)

SCIPIO

Hasdrubal was right. Hannibal has gone mad.
(*He goes to the back to join* DRUSUS.) . . . .

FABIUS

Let this be a lesson to doubters. Hannibal,
with all his elephants and all his men, could not
subdue the high moral purpose of Rome.

AMYTIS

Virtue is rewarded—isn't it, Fabius?

(*The African war drums start beating. The
bugles come in, with a suggestion of wild, barbaric
marching music.*)

FABIUS

Virtue, my dear, is the one perfect defense
against all the evil forces on this earth.

SCIPIO

Look, Fabius—the army has started to move!

(FABIUS *goes to the back and looks off toward
the left.* AMYTIS *remains alone before the column.*)

FABIUS

What a glorious sight!

SCIPIO

There's Hannibal—riding away . . .

(*The terrifying sound of the drums and bugles
swells in volume, the bugles seeming to shriek a*

final message of savage defiance to Rome. . .
AMYTIS *goes to the top of the steps at the back, so
that she is behind* FABIUS *and the others. She
smiles sadly, and waves her hand to the departing
Carthaginians.*)

CURTAIN.